Scott Foresman

Grammar and Writing Practice Book

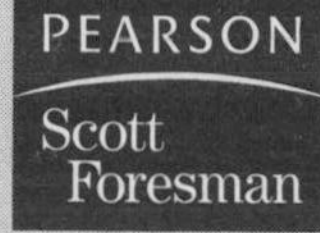

Editorial Offices: Glenview, Illinois • Parsippany, New Jersey • New York, New York
Sales Offices: Boston, Massachusetts • Duluth, Georgia • Glenview, Illinois
Coppell, Texas • Sacramento, California • Mesa, Arizona

ISBN: 0-328-14624-2

9 10 V004 14 13 12 11 10 09 08

Unit 1 Dollars and Sense

Unit 2 Smart Solutions

Unit 3 People in Nature

Unit 4 One of a Kind

Unit 5 Cultures

Unit 6 Freedom

Grammar Extra Practice

Standardized Test Preparation

Unit Writing Lessons

Grammar Lessons

Name ____________________

Sentences

A **sentence** tells a complete thought. It begins with a capital letter and ends with a punctuation mark. An incomplete sentence is called a **fragment.**

Sentence My favorite pie is blueberry.
Fragment Smells so good

Directions Write the group of words that is a sentence.

1. Mom baked a pie for dessert. With red and blue berries.

____

2. The baker worked in the kitchen. Used flour for the crust.

____

Directions Decide whether each group of words is a sentence or a fragment. If it is a sentence, write the sentence with correct capitalization and punctuation. If it is a fragment, write *F.*

3. the trees have green apples

____

4. pick apples for a pie

____

5. the baker puts spices in the apple pie

____

6. on top of the crust

____

Home Activity Your child learned about sentences. Have your child write two or three sentences about an event at school.

Name ______________________________

Sentences

Directions Add your own words to make complete sentences. Write the new sentences. Remember to use capital letters and punctuation marks.

1. _____ went to the gold fields in California.

____

____

2. People on stagecoaches _____.

____

____

3. _____ did many different jobs.

____

____

4. Families of miners _____.

____

____

Directions What do you think the stagecoach ride to California was like? Write three sentences that describe the ride.

____

____

____

Home Activity Your child learned how to use sentences in writing. Have your child write two or three sentences about something he or she saw on the way to or from school.

Name ______________________

Sentences

Directions Mark the letter of the sentence that has correct capitalization and punctuation.

1. **A** Miners wore blue jeans
   B miners wore blue jeans?
   C miners wore blue jeans.
   D Miners wore blue jeans.

2. **A** Jeans were made of denim.
   B jeans were made of denim
   C Jeans were made of denim
   D jeans were made of denim.

3. **A** Does he sell jeans.
   B does he sell jeans?
   C Does he sell jeans?
   D Does he sell jeans

4. **A** Blue jeans are still popular
   B Blue jeans are still popular.
   C blue jeans are still popular
   D blue jeans are still popular.

Directions Mark the letter of the complete sentence.

5. **A** Houses during the Gold Rush.
   B Some miners built houses.
   C Built houses near gold mines.
   D Were simple but cozy.

6. **A** Makes breakfast for miners.
   B Need a big morning meal.
   C Hungry in the morning.
   D One café served hearty breakfasts.

7. **A** The Gold Rush didn't last long.
   B Not find much gold.
   C Families of the miners.
   D Far from home in California.

8. **A** Some miners found gold.
   B In the clear rivers.
   C Work there all day.
   D Men with picks and shovels.

9. **A** Other jobs in town.
   B Stayed there anyway.
   C Families settled down there.
   D Many new people.

10. **A** In rocks along the hills.
    B People still find gold there.
    C Is worth much money.
    D Miners with good luck.

Home Activity Your child prepared for taking tests on sentences. Ask your child to explain the difference between a sentence and a fragment.

Name ______________________________

Sentences

Directions Read each group of words. Write *S* if the group of words is a sentence. Write *F* if the group of words is a fragment.

1. Rode in a stagecoach. ________

2. Families took all their belongings. ________

3. On the range each night. ________

4. Wild animals and diseases. ________

5. After a long journey, they reached California. ________

Directions Decide whether each group of words is a sentence or a fragment. If it is a sentence, write the sentence with correct capitalization and punctuation. If it is a fragment, write *F***.**

6. some miners got rich

____

7. at the bottom of a stream

____

8. panned for gold in the water

____

9. were greedy for more gold

____

10. miners ate in restaurants

____

Directions Add your own words to make a complete sentence. Write the new sentence. Remember to use a capital letter and a punctuation mark.

A California boom town ______.

____

____

Home Activity Your child reviewed sentences. Say some sentence subjects *(Mom, The boy, Some people)* and have your child add words to make a complete sentence.

Name ______________________________

Subjects and Predicates

A sentence has a **subject** and a **predicate.** The subject is the sentence part that tells whom or what the sentence is about. All the words in the subject are called the complete subject. The predicate is the sentence part that tells what the subject is or does. All the words in the predicate are called the complete predicate.

In the following sentence, the complete subject is underlined once. The complete predicate is underlined twice.

The market has many interesting things.

Directions Underline the complete subject of each sentence.

1. Many people buy beautiful carpets at the market.
2. Farmers bring goats to the market too.
3. The vegetables in the stalls look delicious.
4. Children run around the town square.
5. Everything happens at the town market!

Directions Underline the complete predicate of each sentence.

6. A young boy asks for help.
7. The old man is wiser than the boy.
8. The students in a classroom learn lessons all the time.
9. Animals learn differently from people.
10. My parents teach me many lessons.

Home Activity Your child learned about subjects and predicates. Say a sentence. Have your child identify its subject and predicate.

Name ______________________

Subjects and Predicates

Directions Add a predicate to each subject to make a complete sentence. Write the sentence with correct punctuation.

1. A carpetmaker

____

2. Two goats

____

3. A merchant in the village

____

Directions Add a subject to each predicate to make a complete sentence. Write the sentence with correct punctuation.

4. knows many important things

____

5. builds houses and barns

____

Directions Think about a lesson you learned when you didn't expect to. Write four sentences that tell about the lesson.

____

____

____

____

Home Activity Your child learned how to use subjects and predicates in writing. Read a story together. Have your child identify subjects and predicates in story sentences.

Name ______________________

Subjects and Predicates

Directions Mark the letter of the complete subject of each sentence.

1. Everyone in the world needs something.
A Everyone
B Everyone in the world
C needs
D needs something

2. A busy carpenter needs tools.
A A busy
B carpenter needs
C A busy carpenter
D needs tools

3. Goats on a farm need food.
A Goats
B need food
C Goats on a farm
D food

4. People in need ask for help.
A People
B People in need
C ask
D ask for help

5. Someone in the town helps others.
A Someone
B town helps others
C Someone in the town
D helps others

6. Every town needs helpers.
A town
B needs
C Every town
D helpers

Directions Mark the letter of the complete predicate of each sentence.

7. A wise man lives in the village.
A A wise man
B man
C lives
D lives in the village

8. The farmer keeps goats in the pen.
A keeps goats in the pen
B keeps goats
C The farmer
D goats

9. The carpenter built a pen for the goats.
A The carpenter
B built a pen
C built a pen for the goats
D built

10. The spinner made beautiful thread.
A The spinner
B made beautiful
C made beautiful thread
D made

Home Activity Your child prepared for taking tests on subjects and predicates. Say a sentence about your family. Ask your child to identify the subject and the predicate of the sentence. Continue with other sentences.

Name ______________________________

Subjects and Predicates

Directions Underline the complete subject of each sentence.

1. A fable tells an old story.

2. Many fables teach a lesson.

3. Some characters take a journey.

4. Wise men are fable characters sometimes.

Directions Underline the complete predicate of each sentence.

5. A young boy finds a special bean in one fable.

6. A princess finds a prince.

7. A king learns something important.

8. You wrote a clever fable.

Directions Add a predicate or a subject to make a complete sentence. Remember to use capital letters and punctuation marks.

9. A kind merchant in a fable

____

____

10. retold fables many times

____

____

Home Activity Your child reviewed subjects and predicates. Have your child say sentences about fables and folk tales he or she has read. Discuss the subject and predicate of each sentence.

Name ______________________________

Statements and Questions

A sentence that tells something is a **statement.** A sentence that asks something is a **question.**

Statement Jill saved her money. **Question** Did Michael buy a bat?

A statement begins with a capital letter and ends with a period. A question begins with a capital letter and ends with a question mark.

Directions Write each sentence. Add the correct end punctuation. Write *S* if the sentence is a statement and *Q* if the sentence is a question.

1. Jacob got his allowance last week

____

2. He spent some money on a movie

____

3. Does Jacob have any money left

____

Directions Add one word from the box to make each statement into a question. Write the new sentences. Use correct capitalization and punctuation.

can	will	should	do

4. The twins get money for their birthday.

____

5. They spend it on a new video game.

____

Home Activity Your child learned about statements and questions. Have your child make up one statement and one question about an animal he or she likes.

Name ______________________________

Statements and Questions

Directions Use each subject and verb in a sentence. Add words to make the sentence complete. Each item will tell you whether to write a statement or a question.

Example: Statement: I want
I want a new bike.

1. Question: books cost

____

2. Statement: store sells

____

3. Question: parents pay

____

4. Question: you save

____

5. Statement: people spend

____

Directions Write three sentences about a time when you saved money. Include at least one question.

____

____

____

____

Home Activity Your child learned how to use statements and questions in writing. Have your child write a letter to you that includes at least one statement and one question.

Name ______________________

Statements and Questions

Directions Mark the letter of the sentence that is written correctly.

1. **A** Jeremy gave his sister a dollar.
B She needed lunch money
C May I borrow a quarter.
D will you pay me back?

2. **A** Tony is buying a horse
B Is she saving her money?
C her aunt gave her a present.
D Does she have a savings account.

3. **A** Families save for many things
B Will the Longs take a vacation.
C The Cooks need a new car.
D Pat's dad wants to build a deck

4. **A** Is that game on sale.
B will you buy it for me?
C Can we play it together?
D Won't it be fun.

5. **A** I can save a dollar each week.
B I will not buy snacks
C Do peanuts cost that much.
D Mom has fruit at home

6. **A** we saw pennies on the street.
B Who lost their money.
C Jim has a hole in his pocket
D Tanya found a nickel.

7. **A** There is a sale at the store
B that game costs too much.
C You can buy two of these.
D Where is your money.

8. **A** Maya helped Mom buy food.
B how many pears did they buy?
C did they need apples.
D She chose some berries

9. **A** This store sells bread
B it smells so good.
C Mr. Lin is a good baker
D Let's get rolls for dinner.

10. **A** Is that a pet store?
B Do you see that fish.
C can we buy one?
D Do you have a fish tank.

Home Activity Your child prepared for taking tests on statements and questions. Read a story together. Have your child identify statements and questions in the story.

Name ______________________________

Statements and Questions

Directions Write *statement* if the sentence is a statement. Write *question* if the sentence is a question.

1. Did William help his brother mow lawns? __________

2. The neighbors pay them for yard work. __________

3. Garden work can be hard. __________

4. Shall we trim this bush? __________

Directions Write each sentence. Add the correct end punctuation. Write *S* if the sentence is a statement and *Q* if the sentence is a question.

5. You can save money at that store

____

6. Shall we buy school supplies there

____

7. Do they have many notebooks

____

8. There are dozens of different pens

____

Directions Write a statement about what you like to spend money on. Then write a question about saving money.

9. ______________________________

____

10. ______________________________

____

Home Activity Your child reviewed statements and questions. Say *question* or *statement* to your child. Have him or her make up that kind of sentence about a sport.

Name ______________________________

Commands and Exclamations

A sentence that tells someone to do something is a **command.** A sentence that shows strong feelings is an **exclamation.**

Command Pay for your lunch.
Exclamation What a big sandwich that is!

Some commands begin with *please*. Commands usually end with periods. The subject of a command is *you*. The word *you* is not written or said, but it is understood. Exclamations can express feelings such as surprise, anger, or excitement. Exclamations begin with a capital letter and end with an exclamation mark.

Directions Write the sentences. Add the correct end punctuation. Write *C* if the sentence is a command and *E* if the sentence is an exclamation.

1. Please come to our car wash next Saturday

____

2. Wow! This is a great way to earn money

____

Directions Use a word from the box to complete each command or exclamation. Write the new sentences. Use correct capitalization and punctuation.

What	Go	Open	How

3. _____ to the bank after school.

____

4. _____ nice the tellers are!

____

Home Activity Your child learned about commands and exclamations. Have your child make up one command and one exclamation about saving money.

Name ______________________

Commands and Exclamations

Directions Write a sentence for each item. Follow the directions.

1. Write a command that you might say to a dog.

____

2. Write an exclamation about a baby.

____

3. Write a command to a friend.

____

4. Write an exclamation that shows surprise.

____

5. Write a command to a family member.

____

Directions Imagine you won a contest. Write one command and two exclamations about the experience.

____

____

____

Home Activity Your child learned how to use commands and exclamations in writing. Have your child make up one command and one exclamation that he or she might use while playing a game outside.

Name ______________________________

Commands and Exclamations

Directions Mark the letter of the answer that best completes the kind of sentence in ( ).

1. _______ a beautiful bird cage this is! (exclamation)
A What
B what
C What.
D What!

2. _______ us a bird for the cage. (command)
A Show!
B show!
C Show
D show

3. _______ write a check to the store. (command)
A Please!
B Please
C please
D please!

4. You're asking such a low _______ (exclamation)
A price.
B price?
C price!
D price

5. Please put the bird in my _______ (command)
A car.
B car!
C car
D car?

6. What fun it is to buy a _______ (exclamation)
A pet.
B pet
C pet?
D pet!

7. This bird squawks like a _______ (exclamation)
A siren?
B siren!
C siren
D siren.

8. _______ it some birdseed. (command)
A Feed!
B feed!
C Feed
D feed

9. _______ the cage in the corner. (command)
A Put!
B Put
C put
D put!

10. This bird can speak ten _______ (exclamation)
A words.
B words?
C words!
D words

Home Activity Your child prepared for taking tests on commands and exclamations. Have your child write a note about a chore to a family member, including a command and an exclamation. Ask your child to identify each kind of sentence.

Name ______________________________

Commands and Exclamations

Directions Write *command* if the sentence is a command or *exclamation* if the sentence is an exclamation.

1. Find an interesting job. ____________

2. Learn about different kinds of work. ____________

3. What a fun job you have! ____________

4. He's the busiest man I know! ____________

Directions Write the sentences. Add the correct end punctuation. Write *C* if the sentence is a command and *E* if the sentence is an exclamation.

5. What a big stack of dollars you have

____

6. Count the money carefully

____

7. This is the most boring chore in the world

____

8. Spend the money on a vacation

____

Directions Write a command you might give on a vacation. Then write an exclamation you might use on a vacation.

9. ______________________________

10. ______________________________

Home Activity Your child reviewed commands and exclamations. Have him or her recall some commands and exclamations he or she made during the day.

Name ______________________________

Compound Sentences

A **simple sentence** has one subject and one predicate. A **compound sentence** contains two simple sentences joined by a comma and a word such as *and, but,* or *or.*

Simple Sentence	I rode my bike to Dan's house.
Simple Sentence	We rode to the park.
Compound Sentence	I rode my bike to Dan's house, and we rode to the park.

Directions Write *S* if the sentence is a simple sentence. Write *C* if the sentence is a compound sentence.

1. Bicycles are important to people in some countries. _______
2. People in some places do not have cars. _______
3. They ride bicycles to work, and they ride them to the store. _______
4. Bicycles cost less than cars, but they are not cheap. _______
5. Bicycles do not make the air dirty, but cars do. _______

Directions Choose one of the words in ( ) to combine each pair of simple sentences. Write the compound sentences on the lines.

6. Chris rode a bicycle up the hill. It was not easy. (but, or)

____

7. Chris skinned his knee. He bumped his head. (but, and)

____

8. Now Chris can ride to school. He can ride to the park. (or, but)

____

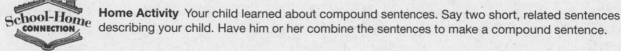

Home Activity Your child learned about compound sentences. Say two short, related sentences describing your child. Have him or her combine the sentences to make a compound sentence.

Name ______________________________

Compound Sentences

Directions Combine each pair of sentences by adding *and, but,* or *or.* Write the compound sentence. Remember to add a comma.

1. Anya saves money to buy a game. I save money to buy a book.

____

____

2. Saving money is hard sometimes. It is worth the effort.

____

____

3. Your parents can buy you a bicycle. You can buy it yourself.

____

____

4. Save a dollar each week. The dollars will add up.

____

____

Directions What would you save money for? Write two simple, related sentences. Then join the sentences to make a compound sentence.

____

____

____

Home Activity Your child learned how to use compound sentences in writing. Have your child write a compound sentence about two things he or she learned today.

Name ________________________________

Compound Sentences

Directions Mark the letter of the words that complete the sentence correctly.

1. Ben walked to the _______ rode.
A game, And David
B game, or David
C game, and David
D game and David

2. There is a path at the _______ is short.
A park, but it
B park, But it
C park, or it
D park and it

3. You can ride in the _______ can ride on the beach.
A hills, but you
B hills, And you
C hills and you
D hills, or you

4. Joel's bicycle is _______ is newer.
A new, or mine
B new, but mine
C new and mine
D new, And mine

5. Skateboards are _______ are fun.
A fast. and they
B fast or they
C fast, and they
D fast, But they

6. We can _______ can ride.
A skate, or we
B skate and we
C skate, And we
D skate but we

7. I can go _______ can go slow.
A fast but I
B fast, or I
C fast, Or I
D fast and I

8. The race was _______ won it.
A hard. but I
B hard or I
C hard and
D hard, but I

9. Ten people _______ finished.
A started, Or five people
B started but five people
C started, and five people
D started. and five people

10. Tim parked in _______ parked in back.
A front, and I
B front, But I
C front, or I
D front and I

Home Activity Your child prepared for taking tests on compound sentences. Have your child find compound sentences in a magazine and identify the two simple sentences that make up each compound sentence and the word that joins the two sentences.

Name ______________________________

Compound Sentences

Directions Write *S* if the sentence is a simple sentence. Write *C* if the sentence is a compound sentence.

1. Katie helps her dad on the farm. ______
2. Katie's dad plants berries, and Katie picks them. ______
3. Sasha's parents own a store, and Sasha helps out there. ______
4. Sasha puts the food on the shelves. ______

Directions Use the word *and, but,* or *or* to combine each pair of sentences. Write the compound sentence.

5. A fair has many things for sale. You can't buy everything.

____

6. You could buy a toy. You could buy a snack.

____

7. One stall sells jewelry. Another stall sells hats.

____

8. Those T-shirts are great. I have many T-shirts at home.

____

Directions Write two sentences about a fair or an amusement park you have visited. Write one simple sentence and one compound sentence.

9. ______________________________

____

10. ______________________________

____

Home Activity Your child reviewed compound sentences. On a walk outside, have your child make up two compound sentences about what you see.

Name ______________________________

Common and Proper Nouns

A **common noun** names any person, place, or thing. A **proper noun** names a particular person, place, or thing. Proper nouns begin with capital letters.

Common Nouns You can see penguins at some zoos.

Proper Nouns In May, Jen saw a penguin from Africa.

Capitalize each important word in a proper noun: Fourth of July. The names of days, months, and holidays are proper nouns. They begin with capital letters.

Directions Write *C* if the underlined noun is a common noun. Write *P* if the underlined noun is a proper noun.

1. There are not many emperor penguins in our country. ________

2. A sea park in San Diego has an emperor penguin. ________

3. In a zoo in Scotland, penguins stroll around the park each day. ________

4. Many people love these unusual animals. ________

5. Whales and penguins are popular sea park attractions. ________

Directions Underline the common nouns and circle the proper nouns in the sentences.

6. Seals and penguins like the cold Atlantic Ocean.

7. Other animals like cold weather too.

8. Will you find bears near the North Pole?

9. Foxes and hares live in Canada.

10. Which bears live in Alaska?

Home Activity Your child learned about common and proper nouns. Have your child write the names of friends and family members and explain why the names are proper nouns.

Name ______________________

Common and Proper Nouns

Directions Rewrite each sentence. Replace each underlined common noun with a proper noun.

1. <u>The city</u> has a zoo with many animals.

____

2. You can get books about animals on a <u>street</u>.

____

3. You can see wild animals at a <u>place</u>.

____

4. Fish live in the <u>river</u>.

____

5. There are many interesting animals in <u>that country</u>.

____

Directions Write a description of a place that has interesting animals. Use at least two proper nouns.

____

____

____

____

____

Home Activity Your child learned how to use common and proper nouns in writing. Look at family photos with your child. Have your child write a sentence about a place your family has visited, using at least one proper noun.

Name ______________________

Common and Proper Nouns

Directions Mark the letter of the sentence that is written correctly.

1. **A** Kelly went to the zoo in San antonio.
B kelly went to the Zoo in san antonio.
C Kelly went to the zoo in San Antonio.
D Kelly went to the zoo in san antonio.

2. **A** Those birds nest in hawaii.
B Those Birds nest in Hawaii.
C Those Birds nest in hawaii.
D Those birds nest in Hawaii.

3. **A** New york city has many pigeons.
B New York City has many pigeons.
C New York City has many Pigeons.
D New york City has many pigeons.

4. **A** My town has many Owls.
B My Town has many owls.
C My town has many owls.
D My Town has many Owls.

5. **A** The robins sing in April.
B The Robins sing in April.
C The robins sing in april.
D The Robins sing in april.

6. **A** Geese and ducks live on the lake.
B Geese and Ducks live on the Lake.
C geese and ducks live on the lake.
D Geese and ducks live on the Lake

7. **A** An eagle flew on the fourth of july.
B An Eagle flew on the Fourth of July.
C An eagle flew on the Fourth of July.
D An eagle flew on the Fourth of july.

8. **A** Many seagulls gathered over the ocean.
B Many Seagulls gathered over the ocean.
C Many seagulls gathered over the Ocean.
D many seagulls gathered over the ocean.

9. **A** Amy drew a turkey for thanksgiving.
B amy drew a turkey for thanksgiving.
C Amy drew a Turkey for Thanksgiving.
D Amy drew a turkey for Thanksgiving.

10. **A** Can birds fly over the washington monument?
B Can birds fly over the Washington Monument?
C Can birds fly over the Washington monument?
D Can Birds fly over the Washington Monument?

Home Activity Your child prepared for taking tests on common and proper nouns. On a drive, say the names of things you pass, such as *a street* and *Spring Creek*. Have your child identify which are common nouns and which are proper nouns.

Name ______________________

Common and Proper Nouns

Directions Write the sentences. Capitalize the proper nouns correctly.

1. We saw the penguins at the zoo on saturday.

____

2. The penguins are from antarctica and south america.

____

3. They are not used to hot summer days in texas.

____

4. Maybe the july sun was too warm for those birds.

____

Directions Underline the common nouns and circle the proper nouns in the sentences.

5. Many animals at the zoo come from distant places.

6. Koalas come from Australia.

7. Pandas come from China.

8. The aquarium brought some whales from the Pacific Ocean.

9. That beautiful tiger was born in India.

Directions Write a sentence about a wild animal. Use at least one proper noun, and circle it. Underline the common nouns.

10. ______________________

____

Home Activity Your child reviewed common and proper nouns. On a walk in your neighborhood, have your child name some common nouns and some proper nouns that name neighborhood sights.

Name ______________________________

Singular and Plural Nouns

A **singular noun** names only one person, place, or thing. A **plural noun** names more than one person, place, or thing.

Singular Nouns The carpenter built a table.
Plural Nouns Workers made desks, chairs, and benches.

Most nouns add *-s* to form the plural. Add *-es* to a noun that ends in *ch, sh, s, ss,* or *x: lunches, dishes, buses, dresses, boxes.* When a noun ends in a consonant and *y,* change the *y* to *i* and then add *-es: bodies.*

Directions Write *S* if the underlined noun is a singular noun. Write *P* if the underlined noun is a plural noun.

1. Tom's father builds houses. _______
2. He puts nails in the walls. _______
3. Tom made a wagon out of wood. _______
4. He put four wheels on the wagon. _______
5. Tom's friends played with the wagon. _______

Directions Write the plural nouns in each sentence.

6. The workers loaded boxes of grapes.

____

7. The trees were full of plump cherries.

____

8. Sarah and her mother will make several pies.

____

9. George picked pears and peaches at the farm.

____

Home Activity Your child learned about singular and plural nouns. Say "I see a [something in your house]" and have your child say the plural form of the word.

Name ______________________________

Singular and Plural Nouns

Directions Complete each sentence by adding plural nouns. Write the new sentence.

1. The workers planted ______ and ______ in the field.

____

____

2. Mrs. Thompson made a salad out of ______ and ______.

____

____

3. ______ and ______ are farm animals.

____

____

4. Workers on a farm use machines such as ______ and ______.

____

____

5. You can buy fresh farm vegetables at ______ and ______.

____

____

Directions Write about workers doing jobs on a farm. Use at least three plural nouns.

____

____

Home Activity Your child learned how to use singular and plural nouns in writing. Have your child write you a note about his or her favorite meal using at least three plural nouns.

Name ______________________

Singular and Plural Nouns

Directions Mark the letter of the plural form of each underlined noun.

1. The workers saw fox in the field.
   A foxs
   B foxes
   C fox
   D foxies

2. The workers cleaned up their mess each day.
   A mess
   B messs
   C messes
   D messies

3. James planted bush in the new garden.
   A bush
   B bushs
   C bushies
   D bushes

4. The men worked in the garden and told story.
   A stories
   B stores
   C storys
   D storss

5. Some played radio all day long.
   A radioes
   B radies
   C radios
   D radio

6. They planted several different grass.
   A grasss
   B grassies
   C gras
   D grasses

7. The garden was full of roses and daisy.
   A daisys
   B daisies
   C daises
   D daisy

8. The workers ate lunch on the bench.
   A bench
   B benchies
   C benches
   D benchs

9. Some bus picked them up after work.
   A buses
   B bussies
   C buss
   D bus

10. They worked in the garden for three week.
    A weex
    B weekes
    C week
    D weeks

Home Activity Your child prepared for taking tests on singular and plural nouns. With your child, take turns naming kinds of insects. Have your child write the plural form of each word.

Name ______________________

Singular and Plural Nouns

Directions Underline the singular nouns and circle the plural nouns in the sentences.

1. The boy helped his grandfather with odd jobs.

2. An uncle cut branches from bushes and trees.

3. His friend put bricks on an old driveway.

4. The cousins fixed two bicycles and a lamp.

5. Many families hired the good workers.

Directions Write the plural form of the noun in ( ).

6. Where would you like to work for two (day)? ____________

7. Would you play with Mrs. Tan's (baby)? ____________

8. You could water Mr. Johnson's pumpkin (patch). ____________

9. Work hard for your (boss). ____________

Directions Write a sentence about a job that could take a day or two to complete. Use at least one singular noun and one plural noun.

10. ____

____

Home Activity Your child reviewed singular and plural nouns. Look at a magazine article with your child. Have your child point out three singular nouns and three plural nouns.

Name ______________________________

Irregular Plural Nouns

A plural noun names more than one person, place, or thing. Most nouns add *-s* to form the plural. An **irregular plural noun** has a special form for the plural.

Singular Nouns A goose and a deer ate a leaf.
Irregular Plural Nouns Some geese and some deer ate some leaves.

Some nouns and their irregular plural forms are *child/children, deer/deer, foot/feet, goose/geese, leaf/leaves, life/lives, man/men, mouse/mice, ox/oxen, sheep/sheep, tooth/teeth,* and *woman/women.*

Directions Write *S* if the underlined noun is singular. Write *P* if the underlined noun is plural.

1. The children had a messy room. _______
2. Aunt Rose would not put a foot into the room. _______
3. There were leaves on the floor. _______
4. I've never seen such a sight in my life! _______
5. Mice could make a nest in there. _______

Directions Write the plural nouns in each sentence.

6. The men on the farm had a problem.

____

7. Deer were eating vegetables from their fields.

____

8. The farmers found holes in the lettuce leaves.

____

9. The women tried to think of clever solutions.

____

Home Activity Your child learned about irregular plural nouns. Say the words *goose, mouse,* and *child* and have your child say the plural form of each word.

Name ________________________________

Irregular Plural Nouns

Directions Write sentences using the plural forms of the nouns.

1. child, tooth

____

2. woman, leaf

____

3. sheep, deer

____

4. goose, mouse

____

5. man, foot

____

Directions Write about a problem you might have in a forest. Use at least two irregular plural nouns.

____

____

____

____

____

Home Activity Your child learned how to use irregular plural nouns in writing. Have your child write a letter or e-mail to a family member about animals he or she has seen. Have your child use at least two irregular plural nouns in the letter or e-mail.

Name ________________________________

Irregular Plural Nouns

Directions Mark the letter of the plural form of each underlined noun.

1. All the <u>child</u> collect something different.
A childs
B childes
C children
D child

2. Carlo has 20 <u>foot</u> of string.
A foots
B feet
C foot
D footes

3. Jo has 8 stuffed <u>mouse</u>.
A mouses
B meese
C mouse
D mice

4. Nick has all his baby <u>tooth</u>.
A teeth
B teeths
C tooth
D tooths

5. Jake has 100 toy army <u>man</u>.
A mans
B man
C men
D manes

6. Maria has 20 plastic <u>sheep</u>.
A sheep
B sheeps
C sheepes
D sheepe

7. Nan has 15 pictures of fall <u>leaf</u>.
A leafs
B leavs
C leaves
D leafes

8. Charlie collects toy <u>deer</u>.
A deere
B deer
C deers
D deeres

Home Activity Your child prepared for taking tests on irregular plural nouns. Have a discussion with your child about the families in your neighborhood. Ask your child to use the singular and plural forms of *man, woman,* and *child.*

Name ______________________________

Irregular Plural Nouns

Directions Underline the singular nouns and circle the plural nouns in the sentences.

1. Neighbors thought the dirty park was a problem.

2. Men cut branches and raked leaves.

3. The children picked up papers.

4. The workers saw several deer and geese during the day.

5. Their feet were muddy, but the park was clean.

Directions Write the plural form of the noun in ( ).

6. A big problem was solved by those (woman). ______________

7. The family's garage was full of (mouse). ______________

8. The ladies brought in cats and (child). ______________

9. Soon the mice ran for their (life). ______________

Directions Write one or two sentences about a clean-up problem and how it was solved. Use the plural forms of at least two of these nouns: *child, foot, leaf, man.*

10. ____

____

Home Activity Your child reviewed irregular plural nouns. Look at a newspaper article with your child. Have your child point out three irregular plural nouns.

Name ______________________________

Singular Possessive Nouns

To show that one person, animal, or thing owns something, use a **singular possessive noun.** Add an apostrophe (') and the letter *s* to a singular noun to make it possessive.

Singular Noun	The hare planted corn.
Singular Possessive Noun	The bear wanted the hare's corn.

Directions Write the possessive noun in each sentence.

1. Aesop's fables tell stories about people and animals. ______________
2. A fox takes a crow's cheese. ______________
3. A mouse frees a lion's paw. ______________
4. A wolf wears a sheep's fur. ______________
5. People enjoy each story's lesson. ______________

Directions Write the possessive form of the underlined noun in each sentence.

6. Jeff favorite fable is about the wind and the sun. ______________
7. The wind challenges the sun power. ______________
8. Which one can remove a man coat? ______________
9. The man feels the wind chill, and he buttons his coat. ______________
10. He pulls up his coat collar. ______________
11. The sun heat makes the man warm, and he takes off his coat. ______________
12. What do you think is the fable lesson? ______________

Home Activity Your child learned about singular possessive nouns. Have your child name objects in your home and use a possessive phrase to tell who they belong to, for example, *Dad's book.*

Name ______________________________

Singular Possessive Nouns

Directions Write sentences about animal stories you know. Use the singular possessive form of each noun shown.

1. animal

____

2. forest

____

3. wolf

____

4. lion

____

5. pig

____

Directions Write two sentences about animal characters. Use at least two singular possessive nouns.

____

____

____

____

____

Home Activity Your child learned how to use singular possessive nouns in writing. Read a story with your child. Have your child write a sentence about the story using at least one singular possessive noun.

Name ___________________________

Singular Possessive Nouns

Directions Mark the letter of the correct possessive noun to complete each sentence.

1. The ____ field needs water.
A farmer
B farmers
C farmer's
D farmers's

2. The ____ sunlight helps the crops.
A day
B day's
C days
D days's

3. The ____ family will help out.
A man's
B mans
C mens
D mans'

4. The ____ soil looks rich.
A cornfields
B cornfield's
C cornfields's
D cornfield

5. The ____ leaves seem healthy.
A lettuce's
B lettuces
C lettuces's
D lettuce'

6. These tomatoes grow in a big ____ shade.
A tree
B trees's
C trees
D tree's

7. The carrots grow near the ____ farm.
A neighbor
B neighbors
C neighbor's
D neighbors's

8. There will be many crops in this ____ harvest.
A falls
B fall's
C falls's
D fall'

9. The family will sell them at the ____ market.
A town's
B towns
C towns's
D town'

10. Then they will plan next ____ crops.
A year
B years
C year's
D year'

Home Activity Your child prepared for taking tests on singular possessive nouns. Have your child think of a friend's name and something that friend owns and make up a sentence using the possessive form of the friend's name.

Name ______________________________

Singular Possessive Nouns

Directions Write the correct possessive noun in ( ) to complete each sentence.

1. Rob played a trick on his (friends, friend's) brother. ____________
2. He put his jacket on (Daves, Dave's) chair. ____________
3. It looked just like the older (boy's, boys's) jacket. ____________
4. The (jackets, jacket's) sleeves were too short for Dave. ____________
5. Dave couldn't believe his (bodys, body's) amazing growth. ____________

Directions Write each sentence. Use the singular possessive form of the underlined noun.

6. Tom put a toy mouse in his <u>sister</u> room.

____

7. His parents heard <u>Annie</u> shouts.

____

8. <u>Tom</u> parents didn't like his tricks.

____

9. His next trick would cost a <u>week</u> allowance.

____

Directions Should people play tricks on others? Answer in a complete sentence. Use at least one singular possessive noun.

10. ____

____

Home Activity Your child reviewed singular possessive nouns. Say the name of a family member. Have your child write a sentence using the singular possessive form of the name.

Name ______________________________

Plural Possessive Nouns

To show that two or more people share or own something, use a **plural possessive noun.**

Plural Noun	The families built houses.
Singular Possessive Noun	The family's house was made of wood.
Plural Possessive Noun	Most families' houses had big fireplaces.

Add an apostrophe (') to plural nouns that end in *-s, -es,* or *-ies* to make them possessive. To make plural nouns that do not end in *-s, -es,* or *-ies* possessive, add an apostrophe and an *s.*

children children's toys women women's books

Directions Write the plural possessive noun in each sentence.

1. With the Indians' help, colonists planted gardens. ______________
2. The gardens' crops included corn and beans. ______________
3. The Americans' first Thanksgiving was special. ______________
4. The settlers' first winters were hard. ______________
5. England's winters were cold, but the colonies' weather was harsher. ______________

Directions Write the possessive form of the underlined plural noun in each sentence.

6. British companies ships brought settlers to America. ______________
7. The ships conditions were not good. ______________
8. Children illnesses were sometimes fatal. ______________
9. Doctors treatments were not very helpful. ______________
10. The travelers hard journey finally ended in America. ______________

Home Activity Your child learned about plural possessive nouns. Name some families in your neighborhood. Have your child make up sentences using the plural possessive form of each noun, such as *The Smiths' dog likes to play ball.*

Name ______________________________

Plural Possessive Nouns

Directions Write sentences about life in America in the 1600s. Use the plural possessive form of each noun in your sentence.

1. farm

____

2. tree

____

3. house

____

4. settler

____

5. colony

____

Directions Write a sentence about something you would have liked about colonial life. Then write a sentence about something you would not have liked. Use at least one plural possessive noun in each sentence.

6. ______________________________

____

7. ______________________________

____

Home Activity Your child learned how to use plural possessive nouns in writing. After watching a movie or TV program, have your child write a sentence about the show that uses at least one plural possessive noun.

Name ______________________________

Plural Possessive Nouns

Directions Mark the letter of the correct singular or plural possessive noun to complete each sentence.

1. Most of the ____ land was full of trees.
A colonys'
B colonie's
C colonys's
D colonies'

2. ____ colony was the first in America.
A Virginias'
B Virginia's
C Virginias's
D Virginia'

3. The ____ hard work cleared the swamp.
A men's
B mens'
C mens
D men

4. They built their ____ homes of wood.
A families
B families'
C familys's
D familys'

5. Those early ____ crops saved the colony.
A farmers'
B farmer's
C farmers's
D farmer'

6. The ____ lives were full.
A colonist's
B colonists'
C colonists's
D colonist'

7. The ____ help was needed too.
A children'
B children
C childrens's
D children's

8. ____ colonists worked hard.
A New England's
B New Englands'
C New Englands's
D New England'

9. The ____ hard work made them successful.
A women
B womens
C women's
D womens's

10. The ____ populations soon grew.
A cities
B citys'
C cities'
D city'

Home Activity Your child prepared for taking tests on plural possessive nouns. Name some kinds of animals. Have your child write sentences using the plural possessive form of each animal name, such as *Zebras' stripes are black and white.*

Name ____________________

Plural Possessive Nouns

Directions Write the correct possessive noun in ( ) to complete each sentence.

1. The early (house', houses') furniture was simple.

____

2. The early (Americans, Americans') meals often included corn.

____

3. The (kitchens', kitchens's) fireplaces served many purposes.

____

4. The (colonists, colonists') clothing was simple too.

____

Directions Write the possessive form of the underlined plural noun in each sentence.

5. The <u>colonies</u> fish and wildlife provided much food.

____

6. <u>Women</u> jobs included cooking and sewing.

____

7. <u>Children</u> games included leapfrog and hopscotch.

____

Directions How is your home like that of an American colonist? Write a sentence to answer. Use at least one plural possessive noun.

8. ____________________

____

Home Activity Your child reviewed plural possessive nouns. Name three things you and your child saw or bought on a recent shopping trip. Have your child spell the plural possessive form of each item name.

Name ______________________________

Action and Linking Verbs

A **verb** is a word that tells what someone or something is or does. **Action verbs** are words that show action. **Linking verbs,** such as *am, is, are, was,* and *were,* do not show action. They link a subject to a word or words in the predicate.

Action Verb We plant flowers in the garden.
Linking Verb The flowers are tulips.

Directions One of the underlined words in each sentence is a verb. Write that word.

1. Amy puts the seed in the ground. ______________
2. She covers it with dirt. ______________
3. It is a pumpkin seed. ______________
4. Pumpkins grow in summer. ______________
5. They are good for decorations. ______________

Directions Write the sentences. Underline the verb in each sentence.

6. Ms. Alvarez grows flowers in a field.

____

7. She sells them at a big market.

____

8. People buy flowers for birthdays and holidays.

____

9. Flowers are bright and cheerful.

____

10. A bunch of flowers is a popular gift.

____

Home Activity Your child learned about action verbs and linking verbs. Have your child name some action verbs that describe what he or she did outdoors today.

Name ______________________________

Action and Linking Verbs

Directions Add a verb to complete each sentence. Write the sentence.

1. Sam's friends ________ in the garden.

____

2. They ________ seeds on the ground.

____

3. Jamie ________ the rosebushes.

____

4. The rose petals ________ as soft as velvet.

____

5. Lucy and Lee ________ a beautiful decoration.

____

6. They ________ the flowers on the table.

____

Directions Write two sentences about a garden. Use one action verb and one linking verb.

____

____

____

____

____

Home Activity Your child learned how to use action verbs and linking verbs in writing. Have your child write a note to you about something that happened at school today. Have him or her circle each action verb and linking verb.

Name ______________________________

Action and Linking Verbs

Directions Mark the letter of the word that is a verb.

1. It rains often in April.
A often
B in
C rains
D April

2. Flowers and trees need much water.
A much
B water
C trees
D need

3. The sun shines every day in June.
A sun
B shines
C in
D every

4. The plants are green and healthy.
A plants
B green
C and
D are

5. Plants grow tall in this season.
A tall
B this
C grow
D season

6. Josh mows the grass each week.
A mows
B week
C each
D grass

7. The weeds on the lawn are brown.
A weeds
B on
C lawn
D are

8. Sharon pulls all the weeds.
A all
B weeds
C pulls
D the

9. Animals and insects like the garden.
A garden
B insects
C like
D the

10. Ants play among the flowers all day.
A play
B day
C all
D flowers

Home Activity Your child prepared for taking tests on action verbs and linking verbs. Have your child make up some sentences about a job that interests him or her. Have your child identify the verb in each sentence.

Name ____________________

Action and Linking Verbs

Directions Underline the verb in each sentence. Write *A* if the verb is an action verb. Write *L* if the verb is a linking verb.

1. Tina wrote a letter to her grandma. ________
2. She told her about her visit with Aunt Maria. ________
3. The visit was short but fun. ________
4. Tina and her aunt took a picnic to the garden. ________
5. The trees in the garden were big and shady. ________

Directions Write the verb in each sentence. Write *A* after each action verb. Write *L* after each linking verb.

6. I am at the museum with Aunt Maria.

____

7. The paintings are unusual.

____

8. We ate lunch at a little café.

____

9. We rode the bus all over the city.

____

10. I was tired but happy.

____

Home Activity Your child reviewed action verbs and linking verbs. Discuss an enjoyable outing your family has had. Have your child write one action verb and one linking verb used in the conversation.

Name ________________________________

Main Verbs and Helping Verbs

A **verb phrase** is a verb that has more than one word. The **main verb** shows action. A **helping verb** shows the time of the action. In the following sentence, *planting* is the main verb, and *are* is the helping verb.

The girls are planting corn with the women.

The helping verbs *am, is,* and *are* show present time. *Was* and *were* show past time. *Will* shows future time. The helping verbs *has, have,* and *had* show that an action happened in the past. In the following sentences, *had* and *will* are helping verbs.

They had planted in spring. We will harvest in fall.

Directions Underline the verb phrase in each sentence.

1. The chief is carving a beautiful pole.
2. He will place it at the entrance of the village.
3. The little boys are learning from the chief.
4. Someday they will carve a pole.
5. They have made many small animals already.

Directions Look at the underlined verb in each sentence. Write *M* if it is a main verb. Write *H* if it is a helping verb.

6. Everyone in the village is helping with the crops. ________
7. The women had planted the seeds. ________
8. The girls have watered the plants. ________
9. The boys are picking the beans. ________
10. The men will plow the fields. ________

Home Activity Your child learned about main verbs and helping verbs. Have your child answer the following question: *What were you doing at 3:00 today?* Then have your child identify the main verb and the helping verb in the answer.

Name ______________________________

Main Verbs and Helping Verbs

Directions Answer each question. Write a sentence with a main verb and a helping verb.

1. What have people made from wood?

____

2. What kinds of trees are growing in your neighborhood?

____

3. Suppose you are a Native American living in the Northwest many years ago. What will you do with a canoe?

____

4. What animals familiar to the Snohomish people have you seen?

____

5. What part of Native American life has interested you the most?

____

Directions Write two sentences about Native American life. Use a main verb and a helping verb in each sentence.

____

____

____

____

____

Home Activity Your child learned how to use main verbs and helping verbs in writing. Ask your child to write a note about something he or she is looking forward to doing in the future. Have your child circle each main verb and underline each helping verb.

Name ______________________________

Main Verbs and Helping Verbs

Directions Mark the letter that shows the main verb in each sentence.

1. Big trees have grown there for ages.
A have
B have grown
C grown
D grown there

2. The people have used wood for many things.
A used
B have
C people have
D have used

3. They are cutting down a fir tree.
A are cutting
B They are
C are
D cutting

4. They will build a house with it.
A They will
B build
C build a house
D will build

5. The young men had made canoes of pine.
A made
B had
C had made
D made canoes

Directions Mark the letter that shows the helping verb in each sentence.

6. I am carving a redwood bowl.
A carving
B am
C I am
D am carving

7. The new bowl will look beautiful.
A will
B will look
C look
D look beautiful

8. A boy is making a bow and arrows.
A is
B boy is
C is making
D making

9. He will use them in the forest.
A will use
B use them
C use
D will

10. We have planted more trees.
A have planted
B planted
C have
D We have

Home Activity Your child prepared for taking tests on main verbs and helping verbs. Have your child make up two sentences about what he or she will do next weekend. Ask your child to identify the main verb and the helping verb in each sentence.

Name ______________________________

Main Verbs and Helping Verbs

Directions Write the main verb and the helping verb in each sentence.

1. The women are sewing animal furs together.

   Main verb: ______________________

   Helping verb: ______________________

2. She is making a coat.

   Main verb: ______________________

   Helping verb: ______________________

3. It will keep someone warm in winter.

   Main verb: ______________________

   Helping verb: ______________________

4. She has created a beautiful hat from bird feathers.

   Main verb: ______________________

   Helping verb: ______________________

Directions Look at the underlined verb in each sentence. Write *M* if it is a main verb. Write *H* if it is a helping verb.

5. The people <u>were</u> celebrating all day. ________

6. They <u>will</u> sing and dance. ________

7. The chief had <u>planned</u> the party. ________

8. The children <u>are</u> playing games. ________

Directions Write a sentence about a celebration. Use a main verb and a helping verb. Underline the main verb. Circle the helping verb.

____

____

Home Activity Your child reviewed main verbs and helping verbs. Ask your child to make up a sentence about a party he or she has attended. Have your child include a main verb and a helping verb in the sentence and identify each.

Name ______________________________

Subject-Verb Agreement

The subject and the verb in a sentence must work together, or **agree.** To make most present tense verbs agree with singular nouns or *he, she,* or *it,* add *-s.* If the subject is a plural noun or *I, you, we,* or *they,* the present tense verb does not end in *-s.*

Singular Subject The bird sings a cheery song. She listens to the music.
Plural Subject The ducks eat the bread crumbs. We watch them.

A form of *be* in a sentence also must agree with the subject. Use *is* or *was* to agree with singular nouns. Use *are* or *were* to agree with plural nouns.

Singular Subject A grasshopper is hiding on the lawn. The ant was busy.
Plural Subject Crickets are singing in the trees. The insects were noisy.

Directions Choose the verb in ( ) that agrees with the subject. Write the verb.

1. The hummingbird (is, are) flying around the garden. ______________

2. Those birds (is, are) so tiny. ______________

3. Moths (are, is) fluttering near the streetlight. ______________

4. A big frog (are, is) croaking at the pond. ______________

5. Some dogs (is, are) answering with barks. ______________

Directions Choose the verb in ( ) that agrees with the subject. Write the sentence.

6. The ants (crawl, crawls) around the picnic table.

____

7. A fly (buzz, buzzes) in the warm air.

____

8. A little spider (makes, make) a big web.

____

Home Activity Your child learned about subject-verb agreement. Have your child tell a sentence about something that happened in school and explain how the subject and verb agree.

Name ______________________________

Subject-Verb Agreement

Directions Use each phrase as the subject of a sentence. Add a verb describing an action that takes place in the present. Make sure each verb agrees with its subject.

1. Some trees

____

2. An inchworm

____

3. Many rocks

____

4. A frisky squirrel

____

5. A bumblebee

____

Directions Write two sentences about snakes. Use verbs that describe actions in the present.

____

____

____

____

____

Home Activity Your child learned how to use subject-verb agreement in writing. Ask your child to write sentences in the present tense about a favorite television program. Have your child circle each verb and explain why it agrees with the subject of the sentence.

Name ______________________________

Subject-Verb Agreement

Directions Mark the letter of the verb that completes each sentence.

1. Kevin ______ rocks from the creek.
A collect
B collects
C collectes
D is collect

2. Each rock ______ beautiful.
A are
B were
C is
D am

3. He ______ a black stone.
A finding
B finds
C find
D findes

4. The stone ______ very old.
A looking
B lookes
C look
D looks

5. His friends ______ the stone.
A wash
B washing
C washs
D washes

6. It ______ getting shiny.
A are
B am
C is
D were

7. Other rocks ______ pink.
A are
B was
C is
D am

8. Kevin's collection ______ each day.
A grow
B growes
C grows
D growing

9. Many people ______ at it.
A lookes
B looks
C looking
D look

10. The hills ______ full of rocks.
A is
B was
C are
D be

Home Activity Your child prepared for taking tests on subject-verb agreement. Point out a sentence in a newspaper. Have your child identify the subject and verb in the sentence and explain why they agree.

Name ______________________________

Subject-Verb Agreement

Directions Choose the verb in ( ) that agrees with the subject. Write the verb.

1. Tamara and Will (are, is) fishing at the pond. ____________

2. Tamara (catches, catch) a fish. ____________

3. The fish (is, are) big and shiny. ____________

4. The children (throw, throws) the fish back. ____________

Directions Choose the verb in ( ) that agrees with each subject. Write the sentence.

5. Jonah (like, likes) trees.

____

6. A big oak tree (grows, grow) in his backyard.

____

7. Robins (is, are) nesting in the tree.

____

8. They (is, are) staying away from the nest.

____

Directions Write a sentence about something in a park that you enjoy. Underline the verb. Make sure it agrees with the subject of the sentence.

____

____

____

Home Activity Your child reviewed subject-verb agreement. Say the names of some people and groups of people in your family and neighborhood. Have your child make up a sentence in the present tense about each with a verb that agrees with the subject.

Name ______________________________

Present, Past, and Future Tenses

Verbs can show when an action happens. This is called **tense.** Different verb tenses have different forms. Many present tense verbs end in *-s.* Form the past tense of many verbs by adding *-ed.* Add the helping verb *will* to a verb to make it a future tense verb.

Present Tense	A whale stays near the beach.
Past Tense	The whale jumped out of the water.
Future Tense	The other whales will jump out soon.

- When a verb ends with *e,* drop the *e* before adding *-ed: glide glided*
- When a one-syllable verb ends with one vowel followed by one consonant, double the final consonant before adding *-ed: shop shopped*
- When a verb ends with a consonant followed by *y,* change the *y* to *i* before adding *-ed: hurry hurried*

Directions Tell the tense of the underlined verb in each sentence. Write *present, past,* or *future.*

1. I like the humpback whales. ______________
2. You will enjoy the whales' music. ______________
3. Those whales traveled from the Arctic Ocean. ______________
4. They will return next year. ______________

Directions Write the verb in ( ) that correctly completes each sentence.

5. Last year Sammy's class (learn, learned) about whales. ______________
6. Whales cannot breathe underwater, so they (jump, jumped) out of the water for air. ______________
7. Each time a mother whale gives birth, she (stays, stayed) close to the baby for a year. ______________
8. After a year, the baby (cared, will care) for itself. ______________

Home Activity Your child learned about present, past, and future tenses. Ask your child to make up a sentence about something he or she saw on the way home from school and identify the tense of the sentence's verb.

Name ______________________________

Present, Past, and Future Tenses

Directions Choose a verb from the word bank to replace each underlined verb. Write the sentence.

chatter	spotted	sails	sprays

1. A boat <u>moves</u> slowly out onto the ocean.

____

____

2. The people on the boat <u>talk</u> excitedly.

____

____

3. Last week the people on the boat <u>watched</u> many whales.

____

____

4. Suddenly, a spout of water <u>jumps</u> out of the ocean.

____

____

Directions Write three sentences about whales. Use present tense in one sentence, past tense in one sentence, and future tense in one sentence.

____

____

____

Home Activity Your child learned how to use present, past, and future tenses in writing. Ask your child to write three sentences about an after-school activity using a different tense in each sentence. Have your child identify the tense of each sentence.

Name ______________________

Present, Past, and Future Tenses

Directions Mark the letter of the verb that completes each sentence. Use the tense in ( ).

1. We ___ for whales in the ocean. (future)
A searched
B will search
C search
D searches

2. Many whales ___ in cold water. (present)
A lived
B will live
C live
D living

3. They ___ to warm water before winter. (future)
A travel
B traveling
C traveled
D will travel

4. Whales ___ in small groups. (present)
A stay
B stays
C stayed
D will stay

5. Those whales ___ a family. (past)
A form
B formed
C forming
D will form

6. They ___ for their babies. (past)
A care
B will care
C cared
D caring

7. That baby whale ___ 2 tons. (present)
A weighs
B weighed
C will weigh
D weighing

8. Its size ___ you. (future)
A will amaze
B amazed
C amazes
D amazing

9. In the past, people ___ whales. (past)
A hunt
B hunting
C hunts
D hunted

10. Most people ___ at whales today. (present)
A look
B will look
C looking
D looks

Home Activity Your child prepared for taking tests on present, past, and future tenses. Point out a sentence in a book you are reading together. Have your child tell whether the sentence is in present, past, or future tense.

Name ______________________________

Present, Past, and Future Tenses

Directions Tell the tense of the underlined verb in each sentence. Write *present, past,* or *future.*

1. A whale lives at the sea park. __________

2. It floats under the water. __________

3. The whale amazed its trainers. __________

4. People will cheer the clever whale. __________

Directions Choose a verb from the list to replace each underlined word or words. Change each verb to the correct tense. Write the sentence.

view leap enjoy

5. A dolphin will jump out of the water.

____

6. Ms. Kenny watched dolphins through the window.

____

7. People like dolphins.

____

Directions Write a sentence about an animal in a sea park. Underline the verb. Tell whether it is present, past, or future tense.

____

____

____

Home Activity Your child reviewed present, past, and future tenses. Say a sentence about the community you live in. Ask your child to identify the verb and the verb tense in your sentence.

Name ______________________________

Irregular Verbs

Usually you add *-ed* to a verb to show past tense. **Irregular verbs** do not follow this rule. Instead of having *-ed* forms to show past tense, irregular verbs change to other words.

Present Tense We do a report on volcanoes.

Past Tense We did a report on volcanoes.

Past with *has, have,* or *had* We have done reports.

Irregular verbs have a special form when they are used with *has* and *have.* Use the special past forms in the third column of the chart only with these helping verbs.

Here are some irregular verbs and their past forms:

Present Tense	Past Tense	Past with *has, have,* or *had*
begin	began	*(has, have, had)* begun
do	did	*(has, have, had)* done
find	found	*(has, have, had)* found
give	gave	*(has, have, had)* given
go	went	*(has, have, had)* gone
run	ran	*(has, have, had)* run
see	saw	*(has, have, had)* seen
take	took	*(has, have, had)* taken
think	thought	*(has, have, had)* thought
wear	wore	*(has, have, had)* worn

Directions Choose the correct form of the irregular verb in ( ) to complete each sentence. Write the verb on the line.

1. Maria has (found, find) a book on Pompeii. ____________________
2. A volcano (go, went) off near the city. ____________________
3. People (run, ran) for their lives. ____________________
4. They (taken, took) all their belongings. ____________________
5. Today many people (see, seen) Pompeii's ruins. ____________________

Home Activity Your child learned about irregular verbs. Ask your child this question: *What did you wear to school today?* Have your child answer with a sentence using *wear* in the past tense (*wore*).

Name ____________________

Irregular Verbs

Directions Write sentences about volcanoes. Use each given word in the past tense.

1. see

____

2. begin

____

3. take

____

4. go

____

5. run

____

Directions Write three sentences describing how a volcano erupted. Use the past tense of at least two irregular verbs.

____

____

____

____

____

____

Home Activity Your child learned how to use irregular verbs in writing. Have your child write a sentence about something your family did on a recent weekend using an irregular verb in the sentence.

Name ______________________________

Irregular Verbs

Directions Mark the letter of the verb that completes each sentence.

1. Curt has ___ a volcano erupt.
A seen
B saw
C see
D sawd

2. The volcano had ___ a big blast.
A gave
B give
C given
D giving

3. The sky ___ getting dark.
A begin
B began
C begun
D beginning

4. Big rocks had ___ out the top.
A go
B went
C going
D gone

5. Lava will soon ___ down the hill.
A ran
B run
C running
D runned

6. People ___ pictures of the eruption.
A taked
B taken
C took
D taking

7. They ___ the sight was amazing.
A think
B thinking
C thought
D thinked

8. Sometimes eruptions ___ many weeks.
A taked
B taken
C taking
D take

9. Volcanoes ___ warnings before a blast.
A given
B give
C giving
D gived

10. People have ___ far from the volcano.
A gone
B went
C go
D going

Home Activity Your child prepared for taking tests on irregular verbs. In a magazine or newspaper, point out a verb. Have your child tell whether the verb is regular or irregular.

Name ______________________________

Irregular Verbs

Directions Write each sentence. Use the past form of the underlined verb. Each new verb will be one word.

1. The Earth <u>gives</u> a big shake.

____

2. Pictures on the wall <u>go</u> crooked.

____

3. The earthquake <u>takes</u> only a few seconds.

____

4. It <u>gives</u> us a little scare.

____

Directions Write each sentence. Use the past form of the verb in ( ) to complete each sentence.

5. We (did, done) a report about the San Francisco earthquake of 1906.

____

6. The earthquake (begun, began) early in the morning.

____

7. Fires had (gone, went) wild in the city.

____

Directions Write a sentence about an earthquake. Use the past tense of an irregular verb. Underline it.

8. ______________________________

Home Activity Your child reviewed irregular verbs. Ask your child this question: *What did I give you for your birthday?* Have your child answer in a sentence using the past tense of *give* (*gave*).

Name ______________________________

Singular and Plural Pronouns

Pronouns are words that take the place of nouns. Pronouns that take the place of singular nouns are **singular pronouns**. *I, me, he, she, him, her,* and *it* are singular pronouns.

Singular Pronoun The man cannot fly. He cannot fly.

Pronouns that take the place of plural nouns are **plural pronouns**. *We, us, they,* and *them* are plural pronouns.

Plural Pronoun Penguins cannot fly. They cannot fly.

You can be used as a singular and a plural pronoun.

Orville and Wilbur, why do you want to fly?
Orville, you will be the first to fly.

Directions Write the pronoun in each sentence.

1. People do not have wings, so we cannot fly. ________________
2. Flying has always interested us. ________________
3. The Wright brothers wanted to fly, so they built an airplane. ________________
4. I have never flown in an airplane. ________________
5. Uncle Joe is a pilot, and he flies often. ________________

Directions Write *S* if the underlined pronoun is singular. Write *P* if it is plural.

6. Inventors were clever, and they made all kinds of flying machines. _____
7. They built wings and attached them to their bodies. _____
8. They made a balloon, and it had a big bucket for passengers. _____
9. We still remember Amelia Earhart. _____
10. She flew all over the world in the early days of airplanes. _____

Home Activity Your child learned about singular and plural pronouns. Make up sentences about one or more members of your family. Have your child repeat the sentences using pronouns in place of people's names.

Name ______________________

Singular and Plural Pronouns

Directions Revise each sentence. Replace the underlined words with singular or plural pronouns.

1. Some people made a kite, and <u>the kite</u> lifted <u>the people</u> into the air.

____

____

2. An inventor made big wings, but <u>the wings</u> could not support <u>the inventor</u>.

____

____

3. An inventor made a glider, and <u>the glider</u> had wings that made <u>the glider</u> sail through the air.

____

____

4. The first airplanes did not have an engine, and <u>the airplanes</u> were heavy.

____

____

5. Orville Wright flew an airplane in 1903, but <u>Orville Wright</u> didn't fly <u>the airplane</u> very far.

____

____

Directions Write three sentences about airplanes. Use at least two different pronouns in the sentences. Underline the pronouns.

____

____

Home Activity Your child learned how to use singular and plural pronouns in writing. Have your child write two sentences about a current event using a singular and a plural pronoun.

Name ______________________

Singular and Plural Pronouns

Directions Mark the letter of the pronoun that can replace the underlined word or words.

1. The Wright brothers built airplanes.
A He
B She
C They
D We

2. A Frenchman flew from France to England in 1909.
A They
B He
C We
D Him

3. Pilots flew airplanes during World War I.
A it
B him
C they
D them

4. Amelia Earhart crossed the Atlantic.
A She
B He
C They
D You

5. Passengers flew many places in 1936.
A He
B She
C They
D Us

6. Nice cabins made passengers comfortable.
A him
B it
C her
D them

7. A flying boat carried people across oceans.
A They
B It
C He
D She

8. Pilots flew jets in the 1950s.
A them
B it
C him
D her

9. A rocket went into space in 1961.
A They
B He
C It
D Them

10. People could really fly!
A It
B She
C Him
D We

Home Activity Your child prepared for taking tests on singular and plural pronouns. Read a book with your child. Point out several sentences with pronouns. Have your child identify the pronouns and tell whether they are singular or plural.

Name ________________________________

Singular and Plural Pronouns

Directions Write *S* if the underlined pronoun is singular. Write *P* if it is plural.

1. An airplane has wings, and they are shaped like a bird's wings. _____

2. The wing is curved, and it helps a bird fly. _____

3. Flaps of the wings move them along. _____

4. The wing's design amazes me. _____

5. Students, you could never invent a wing like this. _____

Directions Write each sentence. Replace the underlined word or words with the correct pronoun.

6. Birds have many different kinds of wings.

____

7. A seagull has long, pointed wings.

____

8. Short, rounded wings help hawks fly.

____

Directions Write a sentence about a bird flying. Use a pronoun. Underline it and write *S* if it is singular or *P* if it is plural.

____

____

____

____

Home Activity Your child reviewed singular and plural pronouns. On an outdoor walk, discuss birds with your child. Have your child identify at least two pronouns used in your discussion.

Name ______________________________

Subject and Object Pronouns

A pronoun used as the subject of a sentence is called a **subject pronoun.** A pronoun used after an action verb or as the object of a preposition is called an **object pronoun.**

- *I, you, he, she, it, we,* and *they* are subject pronouns.
- *Me, you, him, her, it, us,* and *them* are object pronouns.

Subject Pronouns They visited Mount Rainier. Sam and I went too.
Object Pronouns The mountain amazed them. They took pictures of Sam and me.

Directions Write the pronouns in each sentence.

1. She was on a high mountain, and the wind bothered her. ______________
2. In the desert, the sun beats down on you. ______________
3. The Mississippi is a long river, and it has many kinds of fish. ______________
4. The huge waterfall impressed him. ______________
5. He and I watched the tide come into shore. ______________

Directions Write *SP* if the underlined pronoun is a subject pronoun. Write *OP* if it is an object pronoun.

6. Lake Superior is the largest of the Great Lakes. It is also the deepest. _____
7. The lake's size interested us. _____
8. Jamal visited Africa. There he saw the Nile River. _____
9. The rains in the tropical forest drenched them. _____
10. The deep snow on the mountain surprised Tina and him. _____

Home Activity Your child learned about subject and object pronouns. Make up sentences about book and movie characters. Have your child repeat the sentences with pronouns in place of the characters' names.

Name ______________________________

Subject and Object Pronouns

Directions Write each sentence. Replace the underlined words with subject or object pronouns.

1. When some people visited the South Pole, the people wore heavy coats to keep the people warm.

____

____

2. Bob hiked in the desert, and Bob took plenty of water with Bob.

____

____

3. Because the island is very wet, the island has many kinds of plants and animals.

____

____

4. As Jack and Chris climbed the mountain, a guide went with Jack and Chris.

____

____

Directions Write three sentences about a place you think is amazing. Use at least one subject pronoun and one object pronoun. Underline the pronouns.

____

____

____

____

Home Activity Your child learned how to use subject and object pronouns in writing. Ask your child to write two sentences about an interesting place he or she has seen. Have your child use a subject pronoun and an object pronoun.

Name ______________________________

Subject and Object Pronouns

Directions Mark the letter of the pronoun that correctly replaces the underlined word or words.

1. Parrots live in the rain forest.
A Them
B She
C Him
D They

2. The South Pole is home to penguins.
A them
B they
C her
D him

3. The river delighted Maria.
A it
B she
C her
D them

4. A climber reached the peak of Mount Everest.
A She
B Her
C They
D Them

5. Cold winds blasted the mountains.
A they
B them
C her
D it

6. Anna and Sue swam in the ocean.
A him
B her
C he
D she

7. The boys visited the desert.
A Them
B Him
C He
D They

8. Camels carried Mark and Jim.
A I
B them
C him
D he

9. Antarctica is too cold for you and I.
A we
B us
C them
D they

10. You and I will like the rainforest.
A We
B Us
C Them
D They

Home Activity Your child prepared for taking tests on subject and object pronouns. Discuss a visit to a farm or zoo with your child. Have your child identify pronouns in the sentences and tell whether they are subject pronouns or object pronouns.

Name ______________________________

Subject and Object Pronouns

Directions Write *SP* if the underlined pronoun is a subject pronoun. Write *OP* if it is an object pronoun.

1. Sir Edmund Hillary was a climber. He reached the top of Mount Everest.

   _____

2. Tenzing Norgay, a guide, went with him. _____
3. Many climbers go to Everest, and the climb challenges them. _____
4. They use all their strength for the climb. _____
5. You could climb Mount Everest. _____

Directions Choose the correct pronoun for each sentence. Write the sentence.

6. Thomas and (me, I) went to Niagara Falls.

   ____

7. The falls amazed (we, us).

   ____

8. (Him, He) and I took pictures of the crashing water.

   ____

Directions Write a sentence about a mountain. Use a pronoun. Underline it and write *SP* if it is a subject pronoun or *OP* if it is an object pronoun.

____

____

____

____

Home Activity Your child reviewed subject and object pronouns. On a walk or drive, ask your child to find a pronoun on a sign. Have your child tell whether it is a subject pronoun or an object pronoun.

Name ______________________________

Possessive Pronouns

Some pronouns show who or what owns, or possesses, something. This kind of pronoun is a **possessive pronoun.**

Possessive Pronouns *My, mine, your, yours, her, hers, our, ours, his, their, theirs,* and *its* are possessive pronouns.

- This is my gold rock, and that is hers.

Directions Write the possessive pronouns in each sentence.

1. When Tracy visited her granddad, she looked for rocks on his farm.

   ____

2. Her favorite rock was limestone. ______________
3. Its color was pale gray. ______________
4. Her brothers found rocks, and they put them in their granddad's study.

   ____

5. They had a shelf for theirs, and Tracy had a shelf for hers. ______________

Directions Choose the possessive pronoun in ( ) that could replace the underlined words in each sentence. Write the sentence.

6. I found a piece of marble, and the marble's color was pink. (their, its)

   ____

7. Your favorite rock is quartz, and my favorite rock is marble. (mine, my)

   ____

8. Is this quartz the quartz you own? (his, yours)

   ____

Home Activity Your child learned about possessive pronouns. With your child, take turns using possessive pronouns in sentences about objects that family members collect. Have your child identify the possessive pronouns in the sentences.

Name ______________________________

Possessive Pronouns

Directions Revise each sentence. Replace the underlined words with possessive pronouns.

1. Daniel chose certain rocks because <u>the rocks'</u> color was bright blue.

____

____

2. Daniel and Matt spent all day at a creek since <u>the creek's</u> shores were covered with rocks.

____

____

3. Daniel and Matt looked for interesting rocks, and <u>Daniel and Matt's</u> bag was soon full.

____

____

4. Matt found a snowy white rock, which was <u>Matt's</u> favorite.

____

____

Directions Write three sentences about a collection owned by you or someone else. Use at least two possessive pronouns. Underline the possessive pronouns.

____

____

____

Home Activity Your child learned how to use possessive pronouns in writing. Have your child write two sentences about his or her favorite toys. Have your child underline possessive pronouns in the sentences.

Name ______________________________

Possessive Pronouns

Directions Mark the letter of the pronoun that correctly completes each sentence.

1. I have cool rocks in ___ collection.
A him
B yours
C my
D mine

2. My dad gave me a rock from ___ collection.
A mine
B theirs
C his
D ours

3. The rock is odd, and ___ color is orange.
A its
B her
C our
D their

4. Dad taught ___ family about rocks.
A our
B mine
C hers
D its

5. We went to a big hill for ___ first lesson.
A yours
B its
C mine
D our

6. My sister Tara got down on ___ knees.
A mine
B yours
C her
D its

7. She found quartz on ___ first try.
A him
B her
C yours
D mine

8. That is your rock, and this is ___.
A my
B mine
C her
D their

9. You will know a rock by ___ color.
A their
B our
C its
D her

10. Rock collecting is a good hobby, and it could be ___.
A my
B yours
C her
D their

Home Activity Your child prepared for taking tests on possessive pronouns. Play a board game with your child. Have your child identify possessive pronouns used by any player as you play.

Name ______________________________

Possessive Pronouns

Directions Circle the correct possessive pronoun for each sentence.

1. Gems are some of (our, ours) most valuable rocks.

2. (Their, Theirs) favorite gem is bright green.

3. Diamonds are found in (my, mine) state.

4. A ruby is a beautiful gem, and (her, its) color is red.

5. Ruby is my birthstone, and diamond is (her, hers).

Directions Write the possessive pronouns in each sentence.

6. Our grandmother has some beautiful gems in her collection.

____

7. I love the diamond for its brilliant sparkle.

____

8. My brother James likes the rubies and their deep red color.

____

9. Grandma has a gem called a moonstone, and it is her favorite.

____

10. He wanted an emerald, and he received it for his birthday.

____

Directions Revise the sentence. Replace the underlined words with a possessive pronoun.

I found a piece of marble, and <u>the marble's</u> color was pink.

____

____

Home Activity Your child reviewed possessive pronouns. While cleaning a room in your home, ask your child to use possessive pronouns to tell who owns various items.

Name ______________________________

Contractions

A **contraction** is a word made by putting two words together. When words are joined in a contraction, an apostrophe shows where a letter or letters have been left out.

- Some contractions combine a pronoun and a verb: *I + am = I'm; he + is = he's; we + are = we're; you + will = you'll; we + will = we'll; they + are = they're.*
- Some contractions combine a verb and *not: can + not = can't; is + not = isn't; do + not = don't; will + not = won't; are + not = aren't.*

Contractions They're swimming in the lake, but I can't see them.

Directions Write the contraction in each sentence.

1. Watch the Olympics, and you'll see some great swimmers. ______________
2. The Americans think they'll win many medals. ______________
3. I won't miss their big race tonight. ______________
4. I can't believe she broke the world record. ______________
5. Maybe we'll swim in the Olympics someday. ______________

Directions Write the contraction in each sentence. Then write the words that make up the contraction.

6. They're starting the race. ______________
7. Jeremy is in this race, and he's in the first lane. ______________
8. It's important to get a fast start. ______________
9. Isn't a fast turn important also? ______________
10. The other swimmers can't beat Jeremy. ______________

Home Activity Your child learned about contractions. With your child, read an article in a local newspaper. Have your child identify the contractions and the words that make up each contraction.

Name ______________________________

Contractions

Directions Write each sentence. Replace the underlined words with contractions.

1. I am studying the history of swimming.

____

____

2. I learned about a popular stroke of the 1800s, and it is called the Australian crawl.

____

____

3. Johnny Weismuller, an American swimmer, was not happy with the Australian crawl.

____

____

4. He is known for inventing the front crawl.

____

____

5. Now we are all using the front crawl.

____

____

Directions Write three sentences about swimming. Use at least two contractions. Underline the contractions.

____

____

____

Home Activity Your child learned how to use contractions in writing. Have your child write two sentences with contractions about water activities he or she enjoys. Have your child point out the contractions.

Name ______________________________

Contractions

Directions Mark the letter of the correct contraction for the underlined words.

1. Swimming is not difficult.
A isnt
B it's
C isn't
D is'nt

2. You will learn some strokes.
A You're
B You'll
C You'd
D Your

3. They are your arm movements.
A They're
B They'd
C They'll
D Their

4. I will show you a kick.
A I'd
B I'm
C Ill
D I'll

5. It is the most popular kick.
A Its
B It's
C It'd
D It'll

6. Do not forget to breathe right.
A Dont
B Do'nt
C Don't
D Doesnt

7. Breathing will not be hard for you.
A wasn't
B weren't
C won't
D we'll

8. Races are not hard either.
A isn't
B are'nt
C arent
D aren't

9. We are learning the basic strokes first.
A We're
B We'll
C We'd
D Were

10. Then we will swim in races.
A we're
B won't
C we'd
D we'll

Home Activity Your child prepared for taking tests on contractions. Together sort through the mail and have your child find contractions in advertisements and notices.

Name ______________________

Contractions

Directions Write the contraction in each sentence. Then write the words that make up the contraction.

1. I learned a new swimming stroke, and it's called the butterfly.

____

2. Some Olympic swimmers do the butterfly, and they're really fast.

____

3. Michael Phelps does the butterfly, and he's one of the world's fastest swimmers.

____

4. I'm learning to do the butterfly gracefully. ______________

5. I think you'll enjoy the butterfly too. ______________

Directions Write the sentences. Replace the underlined words with a contraction.

6. I learned the breaststroke, and it <u>was not</u> easy.

____

7. I <u>could not</u> move my arms and legs correctly.

____

8. My friend Rosa learned the breaststroke too, and <u>she is</u> good at it.

____

9. I <u>did not</u> get too far with this new stroke.

____

10. From now on <u>I will</u> stick with the backstroke!

____

Home Activity Your child reviewed contractions. Ask your child to answer the following questions using complete sentences with contractions: *Will you go swimming next summer? Would you like to be in the Olympics?*

Name ______________________________

Prepositions

A **preposition** is the first word in a group of words called a prepositional phrase. A **prepositional phrase** ends with a noun or pronoun called the **object of the preposition.** A prepositional phrase tells more about other words in a sentence.

Preposition	The eagle flew <u>in</u> a circle.
Prepositional Phrase	The eagle flew <u>in a circle</u>.
Object of Preposition	The eagle flew in a <u>circle</u>.

Common Prepositions

Here are some prepositions: *about, above, across, after, against, along, among, around, at, before, behind, below, beneath, beside, between, beyond, by, down, during, except, for, from, in, inside, into, near, of, off, on, onto, out, outside, over, past, since, through, throughout, to, toward, under, underneath, until, up, upon, with, within, without.*

Directions Write the preposition in each sentence.

1. Our class read a book about eagles. ______________

2. Bald eagles live in the United States. ______________

3. Bald eagles can grab fish from the water. ______________

4. The bald eagle population decreased during the 1970s. ______________

Directions Write the prepositional phrase in each sentence. Underline the preposition.

5. Another eagle within the United States is the golden eagle.

____

6. Golden eagles have golden brown feathers on their necks.

____

Home Activity Your child learned about prepositions. With your child, look at ads. Have your child identify five prepositional phrases.

Name ________________________________

Prepositions

Directions Add a prepositional phrase to each sentence to make it more specific. Use a prepositional phrase from the box or a prepositional phrase of your own.

through the air	on their tails	in the lake
at the national park	at the library	on high cliffs

1. We saw eagles.

____

2. The eagles had white feathers.

____

3. They glided.

____

4. The eagles built nests.

____

5. The eagles hunted fish.

____

6. We will study eagles.

____

Directions Write two sentences about seeing wildlife. Use at least two prepositional phrases. Underline the prepositional phrases.

____

____

____

____

Home Activity Your child learned how to use prepositions in writing. Have your child write a sentence about a bird that includes a prepositional phrase. Ask your child to point to the prepositional phrase, the preposition, and the object of the preposition.

Name ________________________________

Prepositions

Directions Mark the letter of the word in each sentence that is a preposition.

1. Eagles live throughout the world.
A the
B throughout
C world
D live

2. They build their nests on treetops.
A build
B their
C nests
D on

3. The eagles fly around the lake.
A around
B the
C lake
D fly

4. Eagles eagerly swoop for prey.
A swoop
B for
C prey
D eagerly

5. They spot prey from the air.
A spot
B the
C from
D air

6. They have wings of an unusual size.
A an
B of
C have
D wings

7. They dive quickly to the ground.
A dive
B ground
C the
D to

8. Eagles hunt during the day.
A during
B hunt
C day
D the

9. They rest at night.
A they
B rest
C at
D night

10. Facts about eagles interest me.
A interest
B me
C about
D eagles

Home Activity Your child prepared for taking tests on prepositions. Look through a cookbook with your child. Ask him or her to find three prepositional phrases in a recipe and identify the preposition in each one.

Name ____________________

Prepositions

Directions Write the prepositional phrase in each sentence. Underline the preposition.

1. A chicken has a comb on its head.

____

2. The comb is located above the beak.

____

3. Each type of chicken has a different comb.

____

4. The one with the zigzag comb is a White Leghorn rooster.

____

Directions Choose the preposition in ( ) that makes sense in each sentence. Write the sentence.

5. Chickens and eagles are different ___ one another. (above, from)

____

6. Chickens fly only ___ short distances. (for, below)

____

7. Eagles can soar high ___ the sky. (off, in)

____

8. Chickens often live ___ farms. (on, out)

____

Home Activity Your child reviewed prepositions. Ask your child to use sentences with prepositional phrases to answer these questions: *Where do you do your homework? When do you do your homework?*

Name ______________________________

Adjectives and Articles

An **adjective** is a word that describes a person, place, or thing. Adjectives tell more about nouns. *A, an,* and *the* are special kinds of adjectives called **articles.**

Adjectives Some girls wore long, bright skirts.
Articles A boy wore an awesome shirt to the party.

- The articles *a* and *an* are used only with singular nouns. *A* is used before a word that begins with a consonant sound: *a jacket, a full cup. An* is used before a word that begins with a vowel sound: *an eagle, an orange jacket, an empty cup.*
- Use *the* before singular or plural nouns: *the shoe, the shoes.*

Directions Write the adjective that describes each underlined noun.

1. Many countries have colorful clothing for celebrations. ______________
2. Indian women wear silk dresses. ______________
3. Many Scottish men have plaid kilts for special occasions. ______________
4. In Russia, men put on long coats. ______________
5. Japanese kimonos are made in many colors. ______________

Directions Circle the article in ( ) that correctly completes each sentence.

6. The American Indian wore (a, an) jacket with colorful beads.
7. (A, The) short pants that man is wearing are German.
8. The African man wore (a, an) orange robe.
9. (The, A) Mexican musicians had big hats.
10. The woman from Chile wore (a, an) outfit with a long, white skirt.

Home Activity Your child learned about adjectives and articles. On a walk, ask your child to use adjectives to describe various objects such as a house, a tree, and a dog.

Name ______________________

Adjectives and Articles

Directions Complete each sentence by adding an adjective. Write the new sentence.

1. Everyone wore ___ clothes to the party.

____

____

2. Amy had on her ___ blouse.

____

____

3. The ___ shirt is Kevin's.

____

____

4. Julio and William came with ___ hats on their heads.

____

____

5. Kay's ___ pants made us laugh.

____

____

Directions Write two sentences about your favorite outfit. Use at least two adjectives. Underline the adjectives.

____

____

____

Home Activity Your child learned how to use adjectives and articles in writing. Ask your child to write a sentence about a costume he or she has worn. Have your child use one or more adjectives in the sentence and identify them.

Name ______________________

Adjectives and Articles

Directions Mark the letter of the word that is an adjective.

1. Tim wore his black shoes.
A wore
B shoes
C Tim
D black

2. I wore old sneakers.
A I
B wore
C old
D sneakers

3. I wear cool sandals in summer.
A in
B cool
C wear
D summer

4. Bill wears warm boots in winter.
A warm
B wears
C boots
D winter

5. Kyle found an orange sock.
A found
B orange
C sock
D Kyle

6. Ann's shoes have thin straps.
A thin
B straps
C have
D shoes

7. Do you need more shoes?
A shoes
B you
C need
D more

8. I can run in my new shoes.
A can
B run
C in
D new

9. The Dutch girl wore wooden shoes.
A girl
B shoes
C wooden
D wore

10. The Swiss girl wore shiny boots.
A shiny
B wore
C boots
D girl

Home Activity Your child prepared for taking tests on adjectives and articles. Circle a paragraph in a newspaper or magazine article. Ask your child to count the articles in the paragraph.

Name ______________________________

Adjectives and Articles

Directions Circle each article. Underline each adjective.

1. People have worn many different styles throughout the years.

2. When Aunt Rose was a teacher, she wore long, straight skirts.

3. Grandma wore nice dresses to school.

4. My mom often wore old jeans in the classroom.

5. A popular style in some schools today is a uniform.

Directions Circle the article in ( ) that correctly completes each sentence.

6. People wear different clothes all over (an, the) world.

7. No one needs (a, an) heavy coat in Hawaii.

8. (A, An) overcoat is needed in Russia.

9. You can wear (a, an) shirt with short sleeves all year in Costa Rica.

10. (A, An) extra raincoat comes in handy in England.

Directions Write two sentences describing the clothes you are wearing today. Use at least two adjectives in each sentence. Circle each article and underline each adjective in your sentences.

____

____

____

____

____

Home Activity Your child reviewed adjectives and articles. Discuss the day's weather with your child. Ask him or her to identify some adjectives used in the conversation.

Name ______________________________

Adjectives That Compare

Adjectives are often used to make comparisons. To compare two people, places, or things, you usually add *-er* to an adjective. To compare three or more people, places, or things, you usually add *-est* to an adjective.

Sometimes you must change the spelling of an adjective when you write the *-er* or *-est* form.

Drop final *e*	fine	finer	finest
Change *y* to *i*	easy	easier	easiest
Double final consonant	big	bigger	biggest

Chicago is a bigger city than Baltimore.

New York is the biggest city in the United States.

Directions Underline the adjective that compares in each sentence.

1. San Juan is the largest city in Puerto Rico.
2. Puerto Rico has a warmer climate than New York.
3. Florida is the closest state to Puerto Rico.
4. Miami is nearer to Puerto Rico than New York is.
5. Is New York a busier city than Miami?

Directions Write *C* if the underlined adjective is a comparative adjective. Write *S* if it is a superlative adjective.

6. Maria's family moved from Mexico City to a smaller city. ________
7. Hillside is the smallest town Maria ever saw. ________
8. Her neighborhood has fewer houses than her old neighborhood. ________
9. The streets are wider in Hillside than in Mexico City. ________
10. The people in Maria's new town are the nicest people she has ever met. ________

Home Activity Your child learned about adjectives that compare. Ask your child to describe some television programs using adjectives that compare.

Name ______________________________

Adjectives That Compare

Directions Add a comparative or superlative adjective to complete each sentence. Use a form of an adjective from the box or an adjective of your own. Make any necessary spelling changes. Write the new sentence.

tasty	sweet	rich	salty	spicy

1. The African dish was the ___ dish at the party.

____

2. The beans were ___ than the meat.

____

3. The Spanish dessert was ___ than the dessert I made.

____

____

4. I think Chinese food is the ___ food in the world.

____

5. African chocolate has the ___ flavor I have ever tasted.

____

____

Directions Write two sentences comparing two or more kinds of food. Use at least two adjectives that compare. Underline the adjectives.

____

____

____

Home Activity Your child learned how to use adjectives that compare in writing. Have your child write a note to a friend or family member that includes one or more adjectives that compare.

Name ______________________________

Adjectives That Compare

Directions Mark the letter of the adjective that correctly completes each sentence.

1. Kay's family had a ___ trip from China.
A longest
B long
C most longest
D more longer

2. Mateo's trip from Mexico was ___ than Kay's trip.
A short
B more short
C shortest
D shorter

3. Ana had the ___ trip of all.
A quick
B quickest
C quicker
D quickly

4. Moving was ___ for Jaime than for his brother.
A hard
B harder
C hardest
D more harder

5. Jaime thought Boston was a ___ city.
A greater
B greatest
C great
D most greatest

6. He met the ___ people in the world there.
A friendliest
B friendlier
C most friendliest
D more friendlier

7. Jaime's dad opened a ___ shop.
A newest
B new
C more newer
D most newest

8. The shop sold the ___ dishes in Puerto Rico.
A prettier
B most prettiest
C more prettier
D prettiest

9. The shop had a ___ window than the one next door.
A big
B bigger
C biggest
D more bigger

10. Soon he had many ___ customers.
A happy
B more happier
C happiest
D most happiest

Home Activity Your child prepared for taking tests on adjectives that compare. Have your child find two adjectives that compare in a letter or an e-mail from a friend or family member.

Name ___________________________

Adjectives That Compare

Directions Underline the adjective that compares in each sentence.

1. Alberto had made the biggest choice of his life.

2. He wanted a safer city than the one he was leaving.

3. Some people want a larger house than they had before.

4. Many people seek a healthier way of life than they have.

5. Alberto thinks the United States is the greatest country in the world.

6. He hopes he will be happier there.

Directions Choose the adjective in ( ) that correctly completes each sentence. Write the adjective on the line.

7. The baseball field is (warmest, warmer) in June than in April.

____

8. The Lions have the (younger, youngest) baseball players of all the teams.

____

9. The Lions play on the (greener, greenest) field of all.

____

10. They are playing the (stronger, strongest) team in the whole league.

____

11. Puerto Rico has (nicest, nicer) weather for baseball than New York.

____

12. Professional baseball has a (longest, longer) season than Little League baseball.

____

Home Activity Your child reviewed adjectives that compare. While listening to music with your child, discuss what you like and dislike. Have your child name some adjectives that compare used in the discussion.

Adverbs

An **adverb** is a word that can tell when, where, or how something happens.

Now the movers pack the furniture. (when)
They carry the furniture outside. (where)
They carefully load the van. (how)

- Adverbs can come before or after the verbs they describe.
- Adverbs that tell how something happens often end in *-ly*.

Directions Underline the adverbs in the sentences.

1. Kim's mother often cooks Korean dishes.
2. She chops cabbage carefully.
3. She gently mixes more vegetables.
4. She quickly cooks the mixture on the stove.

Directions Choose the correct word in ( ) to write each new sentence.

5. Everyone (usual, usually) wears costumes to the school party.

____

____

6. Kim (happily, happy) wears her Korean outfit.

____

7. The jacket fits (tight, tightly) around her shoulders.

____

8. The skirt falls (loosely, loose) around her feet.

____

Home Activity Your child learned about adverbs. Ask your child to describe something he or she did today using one or more adverbs.

Name ______________________

Adverbs

Directions Make each sentence more specific by adding an adverb from the box or an adverb of your own. Write the new sentence.

impressively	cautiously	always
really	outside	suddenly

1. Jonah practices Korean martial arts in the mornings.

____

____

2. He likes *tae kwon do*.

____

3. Jonah kicks his legs.

____

4. Jonah and the other class members jump.

____

5. The teacher uses his feet.

____

6. In warm weather, students practice in the courtyard.

____

____

Directions Write two sentences about actions you do in a sport or activity. Use at least two adverbs. Underline the adverbs.

____

____

Home Activity Your child learned how to use adverbs in writing. Have your child write a postcard to a friend or family member and include an adverb in the message.

Name ______________________________

Adverbs

Directions Mark the letter of the word that is an adverb.

1. It rains heavily in Korea in winter.
A rains
B heavily
C in
D winter

2. The monsoon wind blows powerfully.
A monsoon
B wind
C blows
D powerfully

3. The rice grows quickly in the wet fields.
A grows
B rice
C quickly
D wet

4. Farmers soon plant some vegetables.
A soon
B plant
C vegetables
D some

5. Fishermen work there on the coasts.
A work
B there
C on
D coasts

6. They catch many kinds of fish easily.
A catch
B fish
C many
D easily

7. Some farmers grow oranges yearly.
A grow
B some
C yearly
D oranges

8. They patiently raise chickens and pigs.
A patiently
B raise
C chickens
D pigs

9. Today Korea produces much food.
A Today
B produces
C much
D food

10. Korea surely has many resources.
A Korea
B many
C surely
D has

Home Activity Your child prepared for taking tests on adverbs. While reading a book with your child, have him or her describe the actions in a picture using two adverbs in the description.

Name ______________________________

Adverbs

Directions Underline the adverb in each sentence.

1. Often, moving to a new country is difficult.

2. You must leave your friends behind.

3. The houses are built differently.

4. The people dress strangely.

5. Soon you like your new home.

Directions Choose the correct word in ( ) to complete each sentence. Write the new sentence.

6. Kim's grandpa lived (peacefully, peaceful) with Kim's family in Korea.

____

____

7. Kim's grandpa moved (cheerful, cheerfully) to America with the family.

____

____

8. He (kindly, kind) tells Kim a story each night.

____

9. He (usually, usual) tells stories about life in Korea.

____

10. Kim looks forward (excited, excitedly) to her grandpa's stories.

____

Home Activity Your child reviewed adverbs. While playing actively, have your child demonstrate the following movements: running slowly, crawling quietly, and walking carefully.

Name ________________________________

Adverbs That Compare

You can use **adverbs** to compare actions. The *-er* form of an adverb compares two actions. The *-est* form of an adverb compares three or more actions.

Jeremy works hard.

Jeremy works harder than Tom does.

Jeremy works hardest of all the students.

Most adverbs that end in *-ly* use *more* and *most* to make comparisons.

The truck moved slowly.

The truck moved more slowly than the car.

The truck moved most slowly of all.

Directions Underline the adverb that compares in each sentence.

1. Mrs. Alvarez sings loudest of all the employees at the bakery.
2. She bakes faster than Mr. Lane does.
3. The bread dough rises most quickly of all.
4. You must knead bread dough more carefully than other kinds of dough.
5. Mrs. Alvarez has been baking longer than you have.

Directions Circle the correct word in ( ) to complete each sentence.

6. The muffins bake (slower, slowest) than the cinnamon rolls.
7. Mr. Costa works (faster, fastest) of all the bakers.
8. Of all the workers, Tony sings (more cheerfully, most cheerfully).
9. Mr. Costa mixes sweet roll dough (most rapidly, more rapidly) than Tony.
10. The sweet rolls are done (sooner, soonest) of all.

Home Activity Your child learned about adverbs that compare. Ask your child to compare how he or she rides a bicycle to the way a friend rides, using an adverb that compares.

Name ______________________

Adverbs That Compare

Directions Answer each question. Use a comparative or superlative form of an adverb in the box or an adverb of your own in each answer.

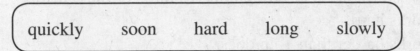

quickly	soon	hard	long	slowly

1. How hard did Carlos and Tara work in cooking class compared to all the other students?

____

____

2. How long did Carlos stay in the kitchen compared to Tara?

____

3. How quickly did Tara mix her cake batter compared to all the other students?

____

____

4. How soon was Tara's cake done compared to Carlos's cake?

____

5. How slowly did Tara's cake rise compared to all the other students' cakes?

____

Directions Write two sentences about experiences you have had helping in the kitchen. Use two adverbs that compare. You may use adverbs from the box above or think of your own. Underline the adverbs.

____

____

____

Home Activity Your child learned how to use adverbs that compare in writing. Have your child write two sentences giving advice about cooking or another activity to someone younger. Have your child use at least one adverb that compares in the sentences.

Name ____________________

Adverbs That Compare

Directions Mark the letter of the word that correctly completes each sentence.

1. Polly's alarm rings ______ than mine does.
A loudest
B loudly
C loud
D louder

2. She is getting up ______ today than yesterday.
A more cheerfully
B cheerful
C most cheerful
D more cheerfuller

3. She will get to the food fair ______ of anyone.
A soon
B more soon
C sooner
D soonest

4. The fair will last ______ this year than last year.
A longly
B longer
C long
D longest

5. Polly will work ______ of anyone at the fair.
A hardest
B hard
C harder
D most hard

6. Of all the workers, she will work ______.
A more quickly
B quicker
C most quickly
D quick

7. She will try new foods ______ than Tim will.
A eagerly
B most eagerly
C more eagerer
D more eagerly

8. She will eat good foods ______ than her friend.
A fast
B more fast
C fastest
D faster

Home Activity Your child prepared for taking tests on adverbs that compare. While working in the kitchen with your child, ask him or her to make up a sentence about cooking that includes an adverb that compares.

Name ___________________________

Adverbs That Compare

Directions Underline the adverb that compares in each sentence.

1. Thomas makes pizza dough faster than Kenneth.

2. Kenneth makes sandwiches more quickly than Thomas.

3. Michael prepares salads earliest of all the chefs.

4. The sandwich is done sooner than the pizza.

5. Which of the three boys worked longest at Mr. King's restaurant?

6. Of the three boys, Michael works most carefully.

Directions Circle the correct word in ( ) to complete each sentence.

7. Of all the students, George worked on his speech (harder, hardest).

8. Jay speaks (loudest, louder) than Katie.

9. Katie speaks (more quietly, most quietly) than the teacher.

10. George talked (more excitedly, most excitedly) of all the speakers.

11. Jay talked (longer, longest) than Katie did.

12. Katie spoke (slower, slowest) of all the students.

Home Activity Your child reviewed adverbs that compare. While driving in the car, have your child compare the actions of some other cars by using the verb *move* and the following words: *faster, fastest, slower, slowest.*

Name ______________________________

Conjunctions

A **conjunction** is a word that connects words or groups of words.

- To add information, use the conjunction *and.* To show a choice, use the conjunction *or.* To show a difference, use the conjunction *but.*
  James went to the park <u>and</u> a ball game.
  James had never been to New York City, <u>but</u> he liked it.
  James could stay in the city <u>or</u> go back home.
- You can use a conjunction to combine two sentences into a compound sentence. Add a comma before the conjunction in a compound sentence.
  James went to a ball game. Then he went home.
  James went to a ball game, and then he went home.

Directions Write the conjunction in each sentence.

1. Railroads were built in the 1800s, and Americans soon depended on them. ________
2. Americans could travel by stagecoach, but trains were much faster. ________
3. People could go 20 miles or all the way across country. ________
4. Today Americans travel by airplanes, cars, and trains. ________
5. You can take a train within a city or between cities. ________

Directions Circle the conjunction in ( ) that best completes each sentence.

6. Daniel saw the Statue of Liberty (but, and) the Empire State Building.
7. Was the Statue of Liberty dedicated in 1884 (or, but) 1886?
8. It was sent to the United States in 1884, (or, but) it was dedicated in 1886.
9. Is the statue made of copper (but, or) marble?
10. The statue was cleaned (but, and) restored in the 1980s.

Home Activity Your child learned about conjunctions. Ask your child to name his or her favorite things to do after school, using one or more conjunctions.

Name ______________________________

Conjunctions

Directions Combine each pair of sentences using the conjunction shown. In combining the pairs, use the underlined repeated words and phrases only once. Make any necessary changes in words. Add a comma in compound sentences.

Example You can see art in a museum. You can see art in a gallery. (or)
You can see art in a museum or gallery.

1. The Empire State Building is a famous skyscraper. The Chrysler Building is a famous skyscraper. (and)

____

____

2. New York City has many parks. James likes Central Park best. (but)

____

____

3. Visitors can go to a baseball game. Visitors can go to a basketball game. (or)

____

____

Directions Write two short, related sentences about a city you have visited. Then combine the sentences using a conjunction. Remember to add a comma.

____

____

____

____

____

Home Activity Your child learned how to use conjunctions in writing. Have your child write two short, related sentences about a recent special occasion in your family. Have your child combine the sentences using a conjunction.

Name ________________________________

Conjunctions

Directions Mark the letter of the word that best completes each sentence.

1. Aunt Kate did not come to my party, ______ Uncle Hal did.
A if
B but
C or
D because

2. Both friends ______ family came to the party.
A or
B but
C nor
D and

3. I got both books ______ games for my birthday.
A or
B but
C nor
D and

4. We can go either for a swim ______ on a picnic.
A but
B and
C or
D with

5. We will eat both sandwiches ______ ice cream at the park.
A and
B for
C or
D but

6. You may have either peaches ______ blueberries on your ice cream.
A but
B or
C because
D and

7. I didn't have a party last year, ______ I had one this year.
A to
B or
C but
D about

8. I can't wait until next year's party, ______ I must.
A but
B since
C or
D from

Home Activity Your child prepared for taking tests on conjunctions. Read a short newspaper article with your child and have him or her point out conjunctions.

Name ___________________________

Conjunctions

Directions Circle the conjunction in ( ) that best completes each sentence.

1. Should we go to the museum (but, or) to the art gallery?
2. That artist's works are not in the museum, (but, or) they are in a gallery.
3. We saw paintings (but, and) collages at the art gallery.
4. The paintings were big (but, and) colorful.
5. Sean's favorites were the paintings, (or, but) mine were the collages.

Directions Use *and, but,* or *or* to combine each pair of short sentences. Remember to use a comma. Write the new sentences.

6. Many artists make collages. This has become a popular art form with students.

____

____

7. I have never made a collage. It's never too late to try one.

____

____

8. I have some bright yarns. They will look good in my picture.

____

____

9. You must use glue carefully. Your collage will be messy.

____

____

Home Activity Your child reviewed conjunctions. While outdoors, have your child make up short sentences about something he or she observes. Then have your child combine the sentences using a conjunction.

Name ______________________________

Capital Letters

Use **capital letters** for proper nouns. Proper nouns include days of the week, months of the year, and holidays. Titles for people should be capitalized when they are used with a person's name. Do not capitalize titles when they are used by themselves.

Incorrect	Last october aunt Rosie and my Uncle gave a party for halloween.
Correct	Last October Aunt Rosie and my uncle gave a party for Halloween.
Incorrect	Does mother's day come earlier than memorial day?
Correct	Does Mother's Day come earlier than Memorial Day?

Directions Write correctly the words that should have capital letters.

1. Last may Mara saw some wonderful sights.

____

2. Mara's mom and aunt lucy took her to the Statue of Liberty.

____

3. They saw the Liberty Bell in philadelphia on memorial day.

____

Directions Write the sentences. Use capital letters correctly.

4. Bartholdi hoped the statue would be finished by july 4, 1876.

____

____

5. Only the statue's arm and torch were ready by the fourth of july.

____

____

Home Activity Your child learned about capital letters. While looking at a magazine, ask your child to point out three capital letters used for days of the week, months of the year, or holidays.

Name ______________________________

Capital Letters

Directions Complete each sentence with a proper noun for the word in ( ). Use capital letters correctly.

1. One of my favorite holidays is ____________________. (holiday)

2. We celebrate this holiday in ____________________. (month)

3. This year my birthday is on ____________________. (day of the week)

4. The day of the week that I like best is ____________________. (day of the week)

5. I like the weather in the month of ____________________. (month)

6. I do not like the weather in the month of ____________________. (month)

Directions Write two sentences about something you do with family members on a particular holiday. Use capital letters correctly.

Home Activity Your child learned how to use capital letters in writing. With your child, recall an event that included many family members. Have your child write a list of the people, using capital letters correctly.

Name ______________________________

Capital Letters

Directions Mark the letter of the word or words that should be capitalized.

1. The family sailed across the ocean in february.
A family
B across
C ocean
D february

2. On monday the children said good-bye to their grandparents.
A monday
B good-bye
C children
D grandparents

3. On friday the ship arrived in a new country.
A ship
B friday
C country
D new

4. The next day aunt sue took her guests to the city.
A next day
B aunt sue
C guests
D city

5. Their aunt told the family about holidays in america.
A aunt
B holidays
C family
D america

6. She said people enjoy fireworks on independence day.
A people
B independence
C independence day
D fireworks

7. Americans remember explorers on columbus day.
A explorers
B voyages
C remember
D columbus day

8. I hope Grandpa visits us at hanukkah.
A hope
B visits
C us
D hanukkah

Home Activity Your child prepared for taking tests on capital letters. Look at a calendar with your child and have him or her point out capital letters and explain the reasons for their use.

Name ______________________________

Capital Letters

Directions If a sentence has capitalization mistakes, write correctly the words that should have capital letters. If a sentence has no capitalization mistakes, write *C*.

1. The Statue of Liberty was repaired in the 1980s. ____________________
2. In our town, mr. barnes raised money for the repairs. ____________________
3. Many Americans helped keep the statue on Liberty Island beautiful. ____________________
4. People celebrated the restored statue on the fourth of july in 1986. ____________________
5. They also celebrated in october, 100 years after the original dedication. ____________________

Directions Write the sentences. Use capital letters correctly.

6. On monday, the class read poems about freedom.
7. A poem by emma lazarus appears on the statue of liberty.
8. Our teacher, ms. adams, says it inspires people from around the world.

Home Activity Your child reviewed capital letters. While outdoors, have your child write the name of a day of the week with correct capitalization using natural objects such as sand, twigs, or pebbles.

Name ______________________________

Abbreviations

An **abbreviation** is a shortened form of a word. Many abbreviations begin with a capital letter and end with a period.

- Some titles used for names of people are abbreviations. For example, *Dr.* is the abbreviation for *Doctor*. The title *Miss* is not abbreviated.

  Mr. Don Lee Chang   Ms. Lucy Ruiz   Mrs. Maya Levin

- An **initial** is the first letter of a name. It is written with a capital letter and is followed by a period.

  Mr. Don L. Chang   L. T. Ruiz   M. E. Levin

- The names of days and months can be abbreviated. *May, June,* and *July* are not abbreviated.

Days of the Week

Sun. Mon. Tues. Wed. Thurs. Fri. Sat.

Months of the Year

Jan. Feb. Mar. Apr. Aug. Sept. Oct. Nov. Dec.

Directions Write each abbreviation. Be sure to capitalize letters and use periods correctly.

1. Mrs W. Wenders ______________________

2. j r Burton ______________________

3. sat, aug 4 ______________________

4. ms T j. Matthews ______________________

Directions Some abbreviations can be used in sentences. Find the word that can be abbreviated in the sentence below. Write the sentence with the abbreviation.

5. Mister Alexis got a pet bird when he moved to this country.

____

____

Home Activity Your child learned about abbreviations. Look through the mail with your child. Have him or her identify abbreviations used for people's names and titles.

Name ______________________________

Abbreviations

Directions Write the answer to each question. Use abbreviations correctly.

1. What are your initials?

____

2. What is the abbreviation for the month in which you were born?

____

3. What are the titles and last names of the adults in your family?

____

4. What is the abbreviation for your busiest day of the week?

____

5. What is the abbreviation for the month in which your favorite holiday takes place?

____

6. What is the abbreviation for today's day of the week?

____

Directions Write two sentences about two adults besides your parents who have taught you important skills or lessons. Use at least two abbreviations.

____

____

____

____

____

____

Home Activity Your child learned how to use abbreviations in writing. With your child, list some adults who live in your neighborhood. Have your child write their names, using the correct abbreviations for their titles.

Name ____________________

Abbreviations

Directions Mark the letter of the correct abbreviation for each word.

1. Monday
A mon
B Mon
C mon.
D Mon.

2. Mister
A mr.
B Mr.
C Mr
D mr

3. April
A Apr.
B apr
C apr.
D Apr

4. Wednesday
A wed.
B wed
C Wed
D Wed.

5. February
A feb
B Feb
C Feb.
D feb.

6. Doctor
A dr
B Dr
C dr.
D Dr.

7. Richard James
A RJ.
B rj.
C R. J.
D r. j.

8. August
A aug
B Aug.
C Aug
D aug.

9. Saturday
A sat.
B sat
C Sat.
D Sat

10. October
A oct
B Oct.
C Oct
D oct.

Home Activity Your child prepared for taking tests on abbreviations. Have your child write the days of the week, using abbreviations correctly.

Name ______________________

Abbreviations

Directions Write each sentence correctly. Use correct capitalization and periods for abbreviations.

1. Dr and mrs Hartz have many beautiful pet birds.

____

2. They will display the birds at the home of mr and Ms Santos.

____

____

3. I am going to see the birds with my friend c. j. Fox.

____

4. You can buy tickets at G B Watkins Department Store.

____

____

Directions The following research notes have initials and abbreviations written incorrectly. Write each note. Correct mistakes in initials and abbreviations.

5. John j Audubon—bird painter

____

6. Born apr 1785

____

7. Wrote book about animals with J Bachman

____

8. Died jan 1851

____

Home Activity Your child reviewed abbreviations. Scan a newspaper with your child and have your child identify abbreviations.

Name ______________________________

Combining Sentences

When you **combine sentences,** you join two sentences that are about the same topic. You make them into one sentence.

- You can join two simple sentences and make a compound sentence. Add a comma and a conjunction such as *and, but,* or *or.*

  Jen painted a tree. I painted a flower.
  Jen painted a tree, and I painted a flower.

- You can combine two sentences that have the same subject.

  Jen painted the sky blue. Jen colored the grass green.
  Jen painted the sky blue and colored the grass green.

- You can combine two sentences that have the same predicate.

  Jen worked on the mural. I worked on the mural.
  Jen and I worked on the mural.

Directions Combine each pair of sentences into a compound sentence. Use a comma and the conjunction in ( ).

1. Some murals show famous people. Our mural shows ordinary people. (but)

____

____

2. I will show you the mural. You can find it yourself. (or)

____

____

Directions Combine the pair of sentences. Use the underlined words only once in the new sentence.

3. <u>Diego Rivera</u> came from Mexico. <u>Diego Rivera</u> painted murals in America.

____

____

Home Activity Your child learned about combining sentences. Point out two short related sentences in a book you are reading with your child. Have your child combine the sentences.

Name ______________________________

Combining Sentences

Directions Combine each pair of simple sentences into a compound sentence. Add a comma and the conjunction *and, but,* or *or*.

1. People painted murals long ago. They still paint murals today.

____

____

2. Some murals are painted outside. Most murals are painted inside.

____

____

3. You can make a mural with paint. You can use bits of glass.

____

____

4. One artist can make a mural. Many artists can work together.

____

____

Directions Write two simple related sentences about murals. Then combine the sentences to make one compound sentence.

____

____

____

____

____

Home Activity Your child learned how to combine sentences in writing. Have your child write two short sentences on the same topic on construction paper, cut them out, and combine them on another sheet of paper, adding a comma and a conjunction such as *and*.

Name ______________________________

Combining Sentences

Directions Mark the letter of the words that complete each sentence correctly.

1. Julia planned a ______ painted it.
A mural, And the class
B mural, or the class
C mural, and the class
D mural and the class

2. The mural is about our ______ is so interesting.
A town, And it
B town, and it
C town, or it
D town and it

3. The mural is not ______ has many scenes.
A huge, but it
B huge, But it
C huge but it
D huge, or it

4. Tim ______ painted the park.
A and Lee
B , and Lee
C and, Lee
D and Lee,

5. You can use yellow ______ can use red.
A paint, Or you
B paint or you
C paint, or you
D paint but you

6. The pictures are ______ bright.
A big, and
B big, and
C , big and
D big and

7. You can paint a ______ can paint a house.
A tree but you
B tree or you
C tree, Or you
D tree, or you

8. People look at the ______ love it.
A mural, or they
B mural, and they
C mural, And they
D mural and they

9. The mural was hard ______ was worth it.
A work, but it
B work but it
C work, But it
D work or it

10. We will paint a mural next ______ will be even better.
A year but it
B year, And it
C year, and it
D year and it

Home Activity Your child prepared for taking tests on combining sentences. Have your child show you pairs of short related sentences from a school paper and explain how to combine them.

Name ____________________

Combining Sentences

Directions Combine each pair of sentences into a compound sentence. Use a comma and the conjunction in ( ).

1. Many painters created murals in the 1960s. This art form is still popular today. (and)

____

____

2. Many murals show real people. Some murals show imaginary characters. (but)

____

____

3. You can paint a mural on wet plaster. You can use canvas. (or)

____

____

Directions Combine each pair of sentences. Use the underlined words only once in your new sentence.

4. <u>That mural</u> shows many different people. <u>That mural</u> pictures several events.

____

____

5. <u>A mural can</u> entertain people. <u>A mural can</u> teach people.

____

____

6. Public buildings <u>are good places for murals</u>. Parks <u>are good places for murals</u>.

____

____

Home Activity Your child reviewed combining sentences. While looking at a magazine or newspaper, ask your child to combine pairs of related sentences in two different ways.

Name ______________________________

Commas

Use a **comma** and a conjunction to join two sentences.

There was a crumb on the table**,** and the ant crawled toward it.

Use **commas** to separate words in a series.

We had sandwiches**,** cookies**,** and fruit at the picnic.

Use a **comma** after the greeting and the closing of a friendly letter.

Dear Jake**,**
Your friend**,**

Use a **comma** between the name of a city and a state in an address.

Chico**,** CA 95926 Berea**,** Kentucky

Use a **comma** to separate the month and day from the year.

July 21**,** 2006

Directions Write *C* if commas are used correctly in the sentence. Write *NC* if commas are not used correctly.

1. Some kinds of ants are army ants, honey ants, and dairying ants. ________
2. Army ants travel in lines and they hunt other insects. ________
3. Dear Amy ________

Directions Write each sentence. Add commas where they are needed.

4. Some ants eat other insects but many do not.

____

____

5. The newspaper had an article about ants on November 14 2005.

____

____

Home Activity Your child learned about commas. Have your child point out five commas in a book that you are reading together.

Name ___________________________

Commas

Directions Answer each question with a complete sentence. Make your writing clear by using commas correctly.

1. In what city and state do you live?

____

____

2. What month, day, and year were you born?

____

____

3. What are three of your favorite colors?

____

____

4. What are three of your favorite foods?

____

____

5. What are two activities you do in your free time? Answer with a compound sentence.

____

____

Directions Write a sentence listing three traits of ants. Use commas correctly.

____

____

____

Home Activity Your child learned how to use commas in writing. Have your child write a sentence naming three animals that he or she likes, using commas correctly.

Commas

Directions Mark the letter of the words that complete the sentence correctly.

1. The ants march along ______.
A grass, bushes, and trees
B grass bushes and trees
C grass, bushes and trees
D grass bushes, and trees

2. The ants carry ______.
A crumbs, salt and sugar
B crumbs salt and sugar
C crumbs, salt, and sugar
D crumbs salt, and sugar

3. Some ants ______ lay eggs.
A work and others
B work, and others
C work, And others
D work And others

4. The ants are ______.
A red black and brown
B red, black and brown
C red black, and brown
D red, black, and brown

5. I drew these ants on ______.
A March 8 2005
B March, 8, 2005
C March 8, 2005
D March 8 2005,

6. I saw many ants in ______.
A Atlanta Georgia
B Atlanta, Georgia
C Atlanta, Georgia,
D Atlanta Georgia,

7. We had a picnic with ______.
A salad, fruit, and juice
B salad fruit and juice
C salad, fruit and juice
D salad fruit, and juice

8. Some ______ came to the picnic too.
A ants bees and flies
B ants bees, and flies
C ants, bees and flies
D ants, bees, and flies

9. Bees ______ crawled.
A flew and ants
B flew, and ants
C flew, And ants
D flew And ants

10. I like ______ doesn't.
A insects but Rob
B insects, But Rob
C insects But Rob
D insects, but Rob

Home Activity Your child prepared for taking tests on commas. Have your child show you some sentences from a school paper or ad and explain why they need commas or not.

Name ____________________

Commas

Directions Fix the comma errors in the sentences in the letter. If a phrase or sentence does not have a comma error, write *C*.

1. Dear Lisa

____

2. We looked at ants bees and butterflies in science class.

____

3. I love butterflies but I am not crazy about ants.

____

4. Tomorrow we will study frogs lizards and snakes.

____

Directions Write each sentence. Add commas where they are needed.

5. My brother went to camp on July 10 2005.

____

____

6. He loves insects and he was happy to live in a tent.

____

____

7. In his tent he saw spiders ants and flies.

____

____

Home Activity Your child reviewed commas. Have your child look at letters and envelopes in the mail and point out commas used in dates and addresses.

Name ________________________________

Quotations

Quotation marks (" ") show the exact words of a speaker in a conversation.

- Use a comma to separate the speaker's exact words from the rest of the sentence.
- Use a capital letter to begin the first word inside the quotation marks.
- Put the punctuation mark that ends the quotation inside the quotation marks.

"I can play music on my pipe**,"** said Elena.
She asked**, "**Shall I play for you?**"**
We replied**, "**That's a great idea!**"**

Quotation marks also indicate many kinds of titles, such as song, poem, and story titles.

We read **"**Elena's Serenade.**"**

Directions Underline the part of each sentence that is a quotation.

1. "I want to play the flute," said Jeremy.

2. "I will teach you," replied Ms. Foster.

3. Ms. Foster said, "Everyone will enjoy your songs."

Directions Write the sentences. Add quotation marks and commas where they are needed.

4. Some of my songs are happy said Jeremy.

____

5. Ms. Foster exclaimed You play beautifully!

____

6. Jeremy can play a song named Paco's Dog.

____

Home Activity Your child learned about quotations. Have your child read aloud a quotation in a book you are reading together and then point out each punctuation mark and explain the reason for it.

Name ______________________________

Quotations

Directions Write a quotation in a sentence to answer each question. Use *I replied, I answered, I said,* and *I exclaimed.*

1. "What is your favorite kind of music?" Jeremy asked.

____

2. "What musical instruments do you know how to play?" Nicole asked.

____

3. "What other musical instrument would you like to play?" Chris asked.

____

4. "What is your favorite kind of dancing?" Anna asked.

____

5. "Why do you like music?" Steven asked.

____

Directions Imagine a conversation you might have with a friend about learning to play a musical instrument. Write three sentences of the conversation. Use quotation marks and other punctuation correctly.

____

____

____

____

____

____

____

Home Activity Your child learned how to use quotations in writing. Have your child write a quotation from a conversation you had during the day. Make sure your child uses correct punctuation marks.

Name ______________________________

Quotations

Directions Mark the letter of the words that should go inside quotation marks.

1. The desert is great, Tim said.
A Tim said
B The desert
C The desert is great,
D The desert is great, Tim

2. Look at the cactus, I responded.
A Look
B Look at the cactus,
C I
D I said

3. Tim said, There are bushes too.
A Tim said,
B Tim said, There
C There are
D There are bushes too.

4. I said, There is not much water.
A There is not much water.
B I said, There
C There is not
D not much water.

5. It is hot and dry, Tim exclaimed.
A Tim said.
B It is hot and dry,
C It is hot
D hot and dry, Tim

6. Do animals live here? I asked.
A Do animals live here?
B Do animals?
C live here? I asked
D I asked.

7. Some like hot weather, Tim said.
A hot weather, Tim said.
B Some like
C Some like hot weather,
D Tim said.

8. I said, I like it too.
A I said,
B I like
C I said, I like
D I like it too.

Home Activity Your child prepared for taking tests on quotations. Have your child identify words in quotation marks in a newspaper article and explain why they are punctuated in that way.

Name ________________________________

Quotations

Directions Write *C* if a sentence is correct. If it is not correct, make the corrections that are needed.

1. Mr. Sanchez said, "You can make beautiful glass by blowing. ______
2. "It is an interesting art," exclaimed Julio. ______
3. You use a blowpipe to make a glass ball," Mr. Sanchez added. ______
4. It looks really hard! Carla said. ______
5. Glassblowing takes a lot of practice," Mr. Sanchez said. ______

Directions Write each sentence. Add a comma and quotation marks where they are needed.

6. People have been blowing glass for thousands of years Ms. Rice said.

____

____

7. She added The blowpipe was invented long ago.

____

____

8. Colonists built a glass factory in Jamestown in 1608 Anita said.

____

____

9. Glassmakers used big furnaces in the 1700s added Ms. Rice.

____

____

Home Activity Your child reviewed quotations. With your child, read aloud a conversation between two or more characters in a favorite storybook and point out and explain the punctuation marks in the dialogue.

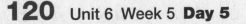

Grammar Extra Practice

Name ___________________________

Sentences

Directions Read the groups of words. Write the group of words that is a sentence.

1. The people on the stagecoach.
The settlers had a hard trip.

____

2. They traveled over high mountains.
Many weeks on the road.

____

3. Good roads had not been built yet.
On the trip from the eastern states.

____

4. Some people got ill on the long journey.
Snakes and wild animals.

____

5. Saw the gold fields for the first time.
The families finally reached California.

____

Directions Decide whether each group of words is a sentence or a fragment. If it is a sentence, write the sentence with correct capitalization and punctuation. If it is a fragment, write *F*.

6. few people had settled in the West

____

7. land with hills and big open spaces

____

8. it was very different from the eastern cities

____

9. built everything themselves

____

Name ________________________

Subjects and Predicates

Directions Underline the complete subject of each sentence.

1. Mom needs help around the house.

2. My little brother needs attention.

3. Everyone in the family needs something.

4. Each person helps the others.

5. All of us think of the needs of others.

Directions Write the complete predicate of each sentence.

6. Julie cooks soup for dinner.

____

7. I wash the car with Dad.

____

8. My brother picks up his toys.

____

9. Each family member has a special job.

____

10. Life at my house goes more smoothly this way.

____

Name ______________________________

Statements and Questions

Directions Write *statement* if the sentence is a statement. Write *question* if the sentence is a question.

1. There is a garage sale down the street. ______________

2. Is that painting for sale? ______________

3. That is a good lamp for my room. ______________

4. Shall we buy this doll for your collection? ______________

5. That old wagon is a real bargain. ______________

Directions Write the sentences. Add the correct end punctuation. Write *S* if the sentence is a statement and *Q* if the sentence is a question.

6. Jeffrey earned two dollars last week

____

7. He got five dollars for his birthday

____

8. Does Jeffrey get an allowance

____

9. He found a dollar in the park

____

10. How much money will Jeffrey save

____

11. Do you think I should buy that game

____

12. I think it's too expensive

____

Name ______________________

Commands and Exclamations

Directions Write *command* if the sentence is a command or *exclamation* if the sentence is an exclamation.

1. Please open a savings account. ______________

2. What a lot of money you've saved! ______________

3. You are the smartest girl at school! ______________

4. Help me save money. ______________

Directions Write the sentences. Add the correct end punctuation. Write *C* if the sentence is a command and *E* if the sentence is an exclamation.

5. Count your birthday money

____

6. What a great toy you could buy

____

7. Save your money for college

____

8. How expensive college is

____

9. Think about your future

____

10. You'll probably get ten scholarships

____

11. That would be wonderful

____

12. Start a savings account today

____

Name ______________________________

Compound Sentences

Directions Write *S* if the sentence is a simple sentence. Write *C* if the sentence is a compound sentence.

1. Many people use bicycles for their jobs. ______

2. Some people deliver messages on their bikes. ______

3. James carries flowers on his bike, and Dave carries groceries. ______

4. Dave prefers heavy loads, but it is hard work. ______

5. Bicycles are fun, and they are also useful. ______

Directions Use the word *and, but,* or *or* to combine each pair of sentences. Write the compound sentence.

6. Kevin worked hard. He saved money for a skateboard.

____

____

7. The store had many skateboards. Kevin wanted a special one.

____

____

8. You buy a skateboard from the store. You order one from a catalog.

____

____

9. Kevin found the perfect skateboard in a catalog. He ordered it right away.

____

____

10. Kevin waited a long time for his skateboard. It was worth the wait.

____

____

Name ______________________________

Common and Proper Nouns

Directions Write *C* if the underlined noun is a common noun. Write *P* if the underlined noun is a proper noun.

1. Antarctica is an unusual <u>continent</u>. ______

2. The <u>South Pole</u> is found there. ______

3. The <u>weather</u> is harsh. ______

4. It is one of the coldest places in the <u>world</u>. ______

5. Yet some animals build <u>nests</u> on the land. ______

6. The islands of <u>Antarctica</u> are home to many birds. ______

7. Some <u>birds</u> live on the ocean. ______

8. They find <u>fish</u> for food. ______

9. Interesting birds live along the seashore of <u>America</u>. ______

10. Gulls and terns nest on the <u>coast</u> and fish at sea. ______

Directions Underline the common nouns and circle the proper nouns in the sentences.

11. Ducks and geese make nests near the North Pole.

12. The animals come to the shores of North America in winter.

13. Many gulls live near the ocean in Canada.

14. They follow ships and eat trash that people throw out.

15. These birds also live on the Great Lakes.

Name ______________________________

Singular and Plural Nouns

Direction Write *S* if the underlined noun is singular. Write *P* if the underlined noun is plural.

1. This neighborhood has many big yards. ______
2. Our yard has a big oak tree and pretty flowers. ______
3. Workers cut the grass in the yards. ______
4. They trim weeds near the sidewalks. ______
5. A gardener plants bushes near a driveway. ______

Directions Write the plural nouns in each sentence.

6. The farmers picked strawberries from the fields.

____

7. The plants grew in long rows.

____

8. They put the strawberries in big boxes.

____

9. The sun was hot, and the workers got warm.

____

10. The boys and girls brought cool drinks to their dads.

____

Name ______________________________

Irregular Plural Nouns

Directions Write *S* if the underlined noun is singular. Write *P* if the underlined noun is plural.

1. The women next door had a problem in their barn. ______
2. Some mice had made homes there. ______
3. The little animals bothered the big oxen in the barn. ______
4. A noisy goose went into the barn. ______
5. Soon there were no mice under the people's feet. ______

Directions Write the plural nouns in each sentence.

6. The children had problems.

____

7. They had loose teeth.

____

8. They could not eat apples or carrots.

____

9. Soon their teeth fell out, and their mouths felt better.

____

10. They could eat snacks again.

____

Name ______________________________

Singular Possessive Nouns

Directions Write the singular possessive noun in each sentence.

1. The little hen used the farmer's wheat for bread.

____

2. The hen asked for each animal's help.

____

3. Each friend's answer was no.

____

4. The animals wanted the hen's good bread.

____

5. The hen enjoyed the bread's taste alone.

____

Directions Write the possessive form of the underlined singular noun in each sentence.

6. What is that story lesson?

____

7. Good bread comes from the baker hard work.

____

8. Everyone wants the worker food.

____

9. No one helps in the cook kitchen.

____

10. Each person help is needed.

____

Name ______________________________

Plural Possessive Nouns

Directions Write the plural possessive noun in each sentence.

1. All the families' houses are different.

____

2. The Smiths' door is red.

____

3. The other neighbors' doors are black.

____

4. The Bradleys' porch is huge.

____

5. The children's toys are there.

____

Directions Write the possessive form of the underlined plural noun in each sentence.

6. The <u>bedrooms</u> furniture came from England.

____

7. The <u>windows</u> panes are made of glass.

____

8. The <u>floors</u> wood is oak.

____

9. The <u>chairs</u> colors are green and blue.

____

10. The <u>women</u> tables are hand carved.

____

Name ______________________________

Action and Linking Verbs

Directions Write the verb in each sentence.

1. Grandma plants bulbs every fall. ____________

2. The plants grow in spring. ____________

3. That plant is a lily. ____________

4. These lilies are white. ____________

5. This bulb is a tulip. ____________

6. Everyone loves Grandma's flowers. ____________

Directions Write the verb in each sentence. Write *A* after an action verb. Write *L* after a linking verb.

7. Peter waters the garden each day. ____________

8. The flowers need special care. ____________

9. Jamal pulls weeds each week. ____________

10. The flowers are prettier than ever this year. ____________

11. The summer rain is important for the flowers. ____________

12. Jessica picks flowers for a special occasion. ____________

13. She arranges roses in a vase. ____________

14. The vase is on the table. ____________

15. Mom enjoys the flowers. ____________

16. She thanks Jessica for the gift. ____________

17. Roses are her favorite flowers. ____________

18. Dad takes a picture. ____________

Name ______________________

Main Verbs and Helping Verbs

Directions Write the main verb and the helping verb in each sentence.

1. The men are hunting for deer in the forest.

Main verb: ______________________

Helping verb: ______________________

2. The women have planted corn in the field.

Main verb: ______________________

Helping verb: ______________________

3. The boys were fishing in the clear lake.

Main verb: ______________________

Helping verb: ______________________

4. The girl has sewn a pretty dress.

Main verb: ______________________

Helping verb: ______________________

5. I am learning about Native American life.

Main verb: ______________________

Helping verb: ______________________

Directions Look at the underlined verb in each sentence. Write *M* if it is a main verb. Write *H* if it is a helping verb.

6. A woman was <u>weaving</u> a basket. ______

7. She <u>will</u> make a necklace with beads. ______

8. The girls had <u>cut</u> the deerskin in pieces. ______

9. They are <u>making</u> shoes for everyone. ______

10. The boy <u>is</u> gathering pretty feathers. ______

Name ______________________________

Subject-Verb Agreement

Direction Choose the verb in ( ) that agrees with the subject. Write the verb.

1. Many animals (come, comes) out at night. ______________

2. An owl (hoot, hoots) high in a tree. ______________

3. A fox (look, looks) for food in the forest. ______________

4. Bats (fly, flies) in the dark sky. ______________

5. Crickets (chirp, chirps) in the garden. ______________

Directions Choose the verb in ( ) that agrees with the subject. Write the sentence.

6. Darkness (is, are) falling on the desert.

____

____

7. Animals (is, are) coming out of their homes.

____

____

8. A jackrabbit (was, were) leaping in the air.

____

____

9. Snakes (crawl, crawls) from under big rocks.

____

____

10. The desert (seem, seems) alive at night.

____

____

Name ______________________________

Present, Past, and Future Tenses

Directions Tell the tense of the underlined verb in each sentence. Write *present, past,* or *future*.

1. Scientists discovered some smart mammals. ____________
2. The mammals live in the ocean. ____________
3. Many dolphins learned tricks. ____________
4. Scientists will study dolphins more. ____________

Directions Write the verb in ( ) that correctly completes each sentence.

5. These dolphins live at the sea park, and they (perform, performed) each day.

   ____

6. A few minutes ago, a dolphin (leaps, leaped) out of the water.

   ____

7. Tomorrow the dolphins (invented, will invent) a new trick.

   ____

8. In next week's show, a dolphin (tossed, will toss) a ball into a net.

   ____

9. Yesterday the dolphins (played, play) happily with their trainers.

   ____

10. I (enjoyed, will enjoy) dolphins in the future.

    ____

11. In yesterday's show, a dolphin (pushed, will push) a ball across the pool.

    ____

12. People watch the dolphins, and then they (clapped, clap) loudly.

    ____

Name ______________________________

Irregular Verbs

Directions Choose the correct form of the irregular verb in ( ) to complete each sentence. Write the verb.

1. That island (begun, began) as a volcano. ____________
2. The scientists had (think, thought) the volcano would erupt soon. ____________
3. Lava (run, ran) down the side of the volcano. ____________
4. We (saw, seen) the eruption, and it looked like fireworks. ____________
5. My dad has (gone, went) to see many volcanoes. ____________
6. He has (took, taken) us to Mount St. Helens. ____________

Directions Write each sentence. Use the correct past form of the verb in ( ).

7. Scientists (find) a volcano in the Pacific Ocean.

____

____

8. They (take) pictures of the volcano.

____

____

9. The scientists (do) a report on the volcano's history.

____

____

10. The volcano (give) the scientists clues about the Earth.

____

____

Name ______________________

Singular and Plural Pronouns

Directions Write the pronoun in each sentence.

1. Have you seen people fly over the ocean? ______________
2. They are parasailing. ______________
3. Eddie has a parachute, and it is attached to a boat. ______________
4. He flies high over the beach. ______________
5. It is a strange way to fly! ______________
6. Sarah drives the boat, and she goes fast. ______________
7. People cheer, but Eddie can't hear them. ______________
8. Sarah gives him a signal. ______________
9. Eddie was watching her. ______________
10. Will Eddie parasail with me? ______________

Directions Write *S* if the underlined pronoun is singular. Write *P* if it is plural.

11. Some people use big kites, and they jump off a high hill. ______
12. The kites carry them through the air. ______
13. Janet jumps, and she glides through the air. ______
14. All of us must take lessons before flying. ______
15. I guess people will invent even more ways to fly. ______
16. Maybe we can think of a new way. ______
17. Dan has an idea, and I like it. ______
18. He will invent a rocket pack. ______
19. Sharon is worried, and Mom agrees with her. ______
20. Dan will try, and I will help him. ______

Name ______________________________

Subject and Object Pronouns

Direction Write *SP* if the underlined pronoun is a subject pronoun. Write *OP* if it is an object pronoun.

1. I visited one of the hottest places in the world. ______
2. We went to Death Valley in the summer. ______
3. The hot sun dazzled us. ______
4. We took plenty of water for Robert and them. ______
5. They took pictures of the desert plants. ______

Directions Choose the correct pronoun to complete each sentence. Write the sentence.

6. My family and (me, I) visited the Grand Canyon.

____

____

7. (We, Us) looked down one mile at the canyon's bottom.

____

____

8. The canyon's colors surprised Jack and (me, I).

____

____

9. Dad and (he, him) rafted on the river at the bottom of the canyon.

____

____

10. Later (they, them) hiked in the park.

____

____

Name ______________________

Possessive Pronouns

Directions Write the possessive pronouns in the sentences.

1. Uncle Rick has valuable rocks on his ranch. ____________

2. Aunt Julie makes her jewelry with the stones. ____________

3. She likes their blue color. ____________

4. Our gifts were made from her purple stones. ____________

5. Mine is a necklace, and hers is a pin. ____________

Directions Choose the possessive pronoun in ( ) that could replace the underlined words in each sentence. Write the sentence.

6. I bought a ring, and <u>the ring's</u> stones are green. (their, its)

____

____

7. The artists showed us <u>the artists'</u> best jewelry. (his, their)

____

____

8. The green stones are the color of <u>Laura's</u> eyes. (hers, her)

____

____

9. Are these earrings <u>the earrings you own</u>? (his, yours)

____

____

10. My necklace is ruby, and <u>Jen's necklace</u> is turquoise. (hers, yours)

____

____

Name ______________________________

Contractions

Directions Write the contraction in each sentence. Then write the word or words that make up the contraction.

1. You can't win the race without training.

____

2. These are Olympic athletes, and they're training many hours each week.

____

3. She's a great swimmer.

____

4. She didn't know swimming was so challenging.

____

5. Maybe you'll become a swimmer too.

____

Directions Write the contraction for the underlined words.

6. You <u>will not</u> believe Gertrude Ederle's strength and will power.

____

7. She <u>could not</u> have crossed the English Channel without them.

____

8. The Channel is wide, and <u>it is</u> stormy.

____

9. Many swimmers have tried to swim the Channel, and <u>they have</u> given up.

____

10. Gertrude Ederle was a great swimmer, and <u>she is</u> my role model.

____

Name ______________________________

Prepositions

Directions Write the preposition in each sentence.

1. The eagle held a fish in its feet. ______________

2. The fish was for the baby eagles. ______________

3. The eagle's nest was high above the lake. ______________

4. The baby eagles' cries filled the air of the forest. ______________

5. The mother eagle landed on the big nest. ______________

Directions Write the prepositional phrase in each sentence. Underline the preposition.

6. These eagles live in Florida.

____

7. They make their homes along the marshes.

____

8. They lay their eggs during the winter.

____

9. The mother bird stays with the eggs.

____

10. The father bird gets food from the water.

____

11. He drops it into the babies' mouths.

____

12. The babies will leave the nest before summer.

____

Name ______________________________

Adjectives and Articles

Directions Circle each article. Underline each adjective.

1. Once, the word *kimono* referred to all clothes in Japan.
2. Then a new piece of clothing was invented.
3. People called the loose outfit a kimono.
4. They loved the bright, colorful kimonos.
5. A kimono was an outfit for both men and women.

Directions Choose the article in ( ) that correctly completes each sentence. Write the sentence.

6. Kimonos had (a, an) advantage over other clothes.

____

____

7. On (a, an) winter day, people could wear many layers of kimonos.

____

____

8. Around 1900, (a, the) people of Japan began wearing styles from Europe and America.

____

____

9. Now, people might wear kimonos for (a, the) wedding.

____

____

10. Kimonos are (a, an) enchanting sight at parties and festivals.

____

____

Name ______________________________

Adjectives That Compare

Directions Underline the adjectives that compare in the sentences.

1. This is the newest neighborhood in town.
2. Families have moved here from the largest and smallest countries.
3. Some of the houses are bigger than others.
4. The Changs' house is the oldest in the neighborhood.
5. All the families are happier in their new homes.

Directions Choose the adjective in ( ) that correctly completes each sentence. Write the sentence.

6. Anna said it is (warmest, warmer) in Virginia than in Russia.

____

____

7. The streets are (busier, busiest) in Moscow than in Williamsburg.

____

____

8. Pilar thinks spring is the (nicer, nicest) season of all in Washington.

____

____

9. The cherry blossoms are the (prettier, prettiest) sight she has ever seen.

____

____

10. It is (coolest, cooler) in Washington than in Spain.

____

____

Name ______________________

Adverbs

Directions Underline the adverbs in the sentences.

1. Luis's family recently moved to a new place.
2. Luis excitedly moved his things into his new room.
3. Next he went to meet his new neighbors.
4. Yesterday Luis saw his new school.
5. He soon got to know the new neighborhood.

Directions Choose the correct word in ( ) to complete each new sentence. Write the new sentence.

6. Maria (sudden, suddenly) felt homesick for her old school.

____

____

7. (Usual, Usually), Maria enjoyed meeting new people.

____

____

8. She sat (quietly, quiet) in class all day.

____

____

9. Some girls (cheerful, cheerfully) asked Maria to play.

____

____

10. She (quick, quickly) felt better.

____

____

Name ______________________________

Adverbs That Compare

Directions Underline the adverb that compares in each sentence.

1. Bread bakes longer than biscuits do.
2. The big oven heats more quickly than the other ovens.
3. Of all the breads, the banana bread will be done soonest.
4. Mrs. Stone kneads dough harder than Kelly does.
5. Of all the neighbors, Mrs. Lopez works most slowly.

Directions Choose the correct word in ( ) to complete each sentence. Write the new sentence.

6. Of all the girls, Jo learned (more quickly, most quickly) how to bake breads.

____

____

7. She worked (hard, hardest) of all on her tomato bread.

____

____

8. Everyone eats her pumpkin bread (faster, fastest) than any other bread.

____

____

9. Uncle Dan compliments Jo (more frequently, most frequently) than I do.

____

____

10. Jo stays in the kitchen (longer, longest) than Mom.

____

____

Name ______________________________

Conjunctions

Directions Write the conjunction in each sentence.

1. Would you rather visit the city or the country on your trip? ____________
2. You can ride horses and have picnics in the country. ____________
3. The country is quiet, but it is interesting. ____________
4. In the city, you can go to museums and cafés. ____________
5. You can ride in buses, trains, or taxis. ____________

Directions Choose the conjunction in ( ) that best completes each sentence. Write the sentence.

6. We went to the museum (but, and) saw all kinds of art.

____

____

7. We saw paintings of people (and, but) buildings.

____

____

8. Most sculptures stand on the floor, (or, but) some hang from the ceiling.

____

____

9. Did you like the paintings (but, or) the sculptures better?

____

____

10. My trip to the museum was educational (but, or) tiring.

____

____

Name ______________________________

Capital Letters

Directions If a sentence has capitalization mistakes, write correctly the words that should have capital letters. If a sentence has no capitalization mistakes, write *C*.

1. In may of 2005, my family flew to Paris, France.

____

2. On tuesday I visited the Eiffel Tower. ______________________________

3. The Eiffel Tower was designed by Alexandre Gustave Eiffel.

____

4. The frame of the Statue of Liberty in new york was also designed by mr. Eiffel.

____

5. Next september, mrs. Austin will take us to see the Statue of Liberty.

____

Directions Write the sentences. Use capital letters correctly.

6. On independence day, Mom called philadelphia.

____

7. On martin luther king, jr., day in january, we went to the Washington Monument.

____

____

8. mr. and mrs. pines drove to plymouth, massachusetts, for thanksgiving.

____

____

9. Dad stopped at Mount Rushmore last memorial day.

____

____

10. On presidents' day in february, Sam visited the Lincoln Memorial.

____

____

Name ______________________

Abbreviations

Directions Write each sentence correctly. Use correct capitalization and periods for abbreviations.

1. On nice days, dr Chin and mr Lee meet at the park.

____

____

2. On Monday, dr Chin brought his son c j and his dog.

____

____

3. Mr and mrs. Lau were at the park also.

____

____

4. They had seen ms Parks and d w Cho there on Saturday.

____

____

5. People brought their birds and cages to l. k. Williams Park.

____

____

Directions Write each telephone message. Correct mistakes in initials and abbreviations.

6. j b Logan called: got your order. ______________________

7. mr Logan, 6 parakeets, jan 10 ______________________

8. Pick up fri, jan 12 ______________________

9. ms Ryan's parakeet, p j ______________________

10. Got bird wed, dec 10 ______________________

Name ______________________________

Combining Sentences

Directions Combine each pair of sentences into a compound sentence. Use a comma and the conjunction in ( ).

1. Our class painted a mural. We worked very hard on it. (and)

____

____

2. We had never painted a mural. It looks great. (but)

____

____

3. Shall I tell you about the mural? Would you like to see it? (or)

____

____

Directions Combine each pair of sentences. Use the underlined words or a form of the underlined words only once in your new sentence.

4. Lewis and Clark sailed up the Missouri River. Lewis and Clark crossed the Rocky Mountains.

____

____

5. The land was a wilderness. The land had not been carefully explored.

____

____

6. Lewis kept a journal of the trip. Clark kept a journal of the trip.

____

Name ______________________________

Commas

Directions Fix the comma errors in the sentences in the letter. If a sentence does not have a comma error, write *C*.

1. Dear Thomas,

____

2. I saw something wonderful and I had to tell you.

____

3. I saw millions of yellow blue and orange butterflies.

____

4. The palm, pine, and fruit trees were full of butterflies.

____

5. Your friend
Justin

____

Directions Write each sentence. Add commas where they are needed.

6. We took a trip to the rain forest on June 23 2005.

____

7. We hiked climbed and rested in the forest.

____

8. We saw incredible plants birds and insects.

____

9. On the ground were fire ants harvester ants and army ants.

____

10. The ants looked dangerous but they left us alone.

____

Name ______________________________

Quotations

Directions Write *C* if a sentence is correct. If it is not correct, make the corrections that are needed.

1. Maria said, "I can have an adventure. ______
2. I will ride a horse to the city! she exclaimed. ______
3. "I will become a famous musician," Maria said. ______
4. "Can you play a flute? Juan asked. ______
5. "No, but I can sing," Maria answered. ______

Directions Write each sentence. Add a comma and quotation marks where they are needed.

6. Maria's mother asked What did you see on your journey?

____

____

7. I saw a clown, a horse, and a flute player Maria answered.

____

____

8. Maria's mother asked How long was your trip?

____

____

9. Maria replied I went a thousand miles, and I was gone a thousand days.

____

____

10. I'm so glad you came back! Maria's mother exclaimed.

____

____

Standardized Test Preparation

Name ______________________________

Language Test

Read the passage. Decide which type of mistake, if any, appears in each underlined section. Mark the letter of your answer.

Did you ever have a great idea for a business. (1) Last summer my friend corey and I (2) started a pet-sitting business. Soon had three customers. (3) We cared for a goldfish, a gray cat, and a little poodel. (4) Each day we walked the poodle, let the cat out of the Smiths house, (5) and fed the fish. We just hoped we didn't get mixed up. We didn't want to let the fish out of the house or put a leash on the cat! (6)

1. **A** Spelling
   B Capitalization
   C Punctuation
   D No mistake

2. **F** Spelling
   G Capitalization
   H Punctuation
   J No mistake

3. **A** Incorrect plural noun
   B Incorrect possessive noun
   C Missing sentence part
   D No mistake

4. **F** Spelling
   G Capitalization
   H Punctuation
   J No mistake

5. **A** Incorrect plural noun
   B Incorrect possessive noun
   C Missing sentence part
   D No mistake

6. **F** Spelling
   G Capitalization
   H Punctuation
   J No mistake

Name ______________________________

Writing Test

Read the paragraph and answer questions 1–4.

(1) You can easily make a pretty flower arrangement. (2) Get several flowers such as tulips or roses. (3) Your parents might let you pick flowers from your yard, or you can buy them from the supermarket. (4) Fill a vase with cool water. (5) Cut at least one inch from the stem of each flower. (6) Arrange the flowers in kind of a pattern or something so the shapes and colors look pleasing. (7) Put your flowers in a place where everyone can enjoy them!

1. Which time-order word would be best to begin sentence 4?

A Yesterday

B Next

C Third

D Finally

2. Which sentence is the best revision of sentence 6?

F Arrange the flowers in kind of a pattern so the shapes and colors look pleasing.

G Arrange the flowers in kind of a pattern or something.

H Arrange the flowers.

J Arrange the flowers so the shapes and colors look pleasing.

3. Which word would be best to replace *Put* in sentence 7?

A Place

B Display

C Lay down

D Toss

4. What is the purpose of this paragraph?

F to persuade readers to take an action

G to explain how to do something

H to make readers laugh

J to give readers important facts

Name ______________________________

Language Test

Read the passage. Decide which type of mistake, if any, appears in each underlined section. Mark the letter of your answer.

Glacier National Park and Yellowstone National Park are both beautifull outdoor places. (1) Glacier National Park has high mountains and valleys of wildflowers. (2) You'll found lakes as clear as glass there. (3) Yellowstone's mountains arent as high, (4) but the park has many wild animals like elk and bison. Smaller animals and them roam (5) freely. Both parks gives (6) visitors many sights to enjoy.

1. A Spelling
   B Capitalization
   C Punctuation
   D No mistake

2. F Spelling
   G Capitalization
   H Punctuation
   J No mistake

3. A Incorrect verb use
   B Incorrect contraction use
   C Incorrect pronoun use
   D No mistake

4. F Incorrect verb use
   G Incorrect contraction use
   H Incorrect pronoun use
   J No mistake

5. A Incorrect verb use
   B Incorrect contraction use
   C Incorrect pronoun use
   D No mistake

6. F Incorrect verb use
   G Incorrect contraction use
   H Incorrect pronoun use
   J No mistake

Writing Test

Read the paragraph and answer questions 1–4.

(1) Annie Smith Peck was an unusual woman. (2) In the 1800s, women did not climb mountains. (3) But Annie had already gone up huge mountains in Europe and North America from 1895–1897. (4) Men also climbed these mountains. (5) She wanted to reach the peak of the highest mountain in Peru. (6) She made many tries over the next few years but had to turn back each time. (7) In 1908, Peck safely reached the highest point in Peru.

1. Which sentence should be left out of this paragraph?

A Sentence 1

B Sentence 2

C Sentence 4

D Sentence 5

2. Which word would be best to replace *gone* in sentence 3?

F scurried

G climbed

H strolled

J got

3. Which time-order word would best begin sentence 5?

A First

B Once

C Second

D Next

4. Which of the following sentences has sensory details that could be used for elaboration after sentence 7?

F Annie climbed nearly 20,000 feet.

G The mountain is about 100 miles from the Pacific coast.

H Peck fought icy slopes and blasting winds on the way down the mountain.

J The Matterhorn has an unusual pointed peak.

Name ______________________________

Language Test

Read the passage. Decide which type of mistake, if any, appears in each underlined section. Mark the letter of your answer.

Cooking dishes from other countries is a great way to learn about other culchures. (1) You can start with tacos, a Mexican dish. (2) Pizza, one of the most popular Italian dishes, makes a delicious friday night meal. (3) Mom makes seafood stews from both Spain and Portugal, but the one from Spain is the tastiest of the two. (4) You don't need to travel to create a international adventure. (5) Just cook delicious foods from around the world for you your family and your friends. (6)

1. **A** Spelling
   B Capitalization
   C Punctuation
   D No mistake

2. **F** Spelling
   G Capitalization
   H Punctuation
   J No mistake

3. **A** Spelling
   B Capitalization
   C Punctuation
   D No mistake

4. **F** Incorrect article use
   G Incorrect adjective use
   H Incorrect adverb use
   J No mistake

5. **A** Incorrect article use
   B Incorrect verb use
   C Incorrect adverb use
   D No mistake

6. **F** Spelling
   G Capitalization
   H Punctuation
   J No mistake

Name ____________________

Writing Test

Read the paragraph and answer questions 1–4.

(1) Martin Luther King, Jr., fought for the freedom of all people. (2) King thought African Americans should have the same rights as other Americans. (3) However, he did not believe in using violence to gain rights. (4) He led peaceful protests. (5) He led a march in Washington that included about 250,000 people. (6) In his speech that day, King told of his dream that all people would finally join hands and sing, "Free at last!"

1. Which would be the best elaboration for sentence 4?

A For example, black and white protesters staged "sit-ins" in places where blacks were not allowed.

B A peaceful protest doesn't have fighting and stuff.

C President Johnson signed the Voting Rights Act to help African Americans vote safely in 1965.

D Many high school and college students attended protests.

2. Which adjective would be the best choice to describe *march* in sentence 5?

F big

G remarkable

H greatest

J interesting

3. Which is the best paraphrase of the paragraph?

A Martin Luther King, Jr., did not believe in violence.

B Martin Luther King, Jr., told of his dream that all people would be free at last.

C About 250,000 people attended a march in Washington.

D Martin Luther King, Jr., used many peaceful methods to help all Americans gain equal rights.

4. What method does the writer use for the conclusion of the paragraph?

F Sum up the main idea.

G Ask a question.

H Use a quotation.

J End with an opinion.

Unit Writing Lessons

Name ______________________________

Notes for a Personal Narrative

Directions Fill in the graphic organizer with information about the event or experience that you plan to write about.

Summary

What happened? ______________________________

When? ______________________________

Where? ______________________________

Who was there? ______________________________

Details

Beginning

Middle

End

Name ____________________

Words That Tell About *You*

Directions How did you feel about your experience at the beginning, middle, and end? Choose one or two words from the word bank to describe each part of your experience. Then add details that *show* readers each feeling.

worried	excited	proud	sad
disappointed	embarrassed	satisfied	curious
puzzled	anxious	delighted	upset

Beginning ____________________

____

____

____

Middle ____________________

____

____

____

End ____________________

____

____

____

Name ______________________________

Elaboration

Combine Sentences

When you write, you can elaborate by combining short, choppy simple sentences to make compound sentences. The two sentences you combine must make sense together. You can combine the sentences using the word *and, but,* or *or.*

Directions Use the word in ( ) to combine the two sentences. Remember to capitalize the first word of the new sentence and to replace the first period with a comma.

1. (but) Many huge weeds grew in the garden. I pulled each weed out.

____

____

2. (and) The job was hard. It took me all afternoon.

____

____

3. (or) Pull out the weed's root. The weed will grow back.

____

____

4. (and) I earned five dollars. I felt good about my hard work.

____

____

5. (but) I was tired. The garden looked great.

____

____

Name ______________________________

Self-Evaluation Guide

Personal Narrative

Directions Think about the final draft of your personal narrative. Then rate yourself on a score of from 4 to 1 (4 is the highest) on each writing trait. After you fill out the chart, answer the questions.

Writing Traits	4	3	2	1
Focus/Ideas				
Organization/Paragraphs				
Voice				
Word Choice				
Sentences				
Conventions				

1. What is the best part of your personal narrative?

____

____

____

____

2. Write one thing you would change about this personal narrative if you had the chance to write it again.

____

____

____

____

Name ______________________________

How-to Chart

Directions Fill in the graphic organizer with information about your project.

Task ______________________________

Materials ______________________________

Introduction ______________________________

____

____

____

____

Steps ______________________________

____

____

____

____

Conclusion ______________________________

____

____

____

____

Name ______________________________

Time-Order Words

Directions Add a time-order word to each of the five steps below. Write each sentence. Then add a final sentence using a time-order word. Tell what you could do with the flowers.

1. Find a pretty vase.

____

____

2. Pick some wildflowers from a field.

____

____

3. Put water in the vase.

____

____

4. Place the flowers in the water.

____

____

5. Arrange the flowers in an attractive pattern.

____

____

6. ______________________________

____

Name ______________________

Elaboration

Vivid Words

When you write, you can elaborate by using vivid, precise words. For example, you can use specific common nouns and proper nouns.

General Words Watch that kite go in the air.
Precise Words Watch that kite soar up in the clouds.

Directions Replace each underlined word with a vivid, precise word. Write each sentence.

1. Cut paper for your kite in a shape.

____

____

2. Make your kite a good color.

____

____

3. Put some sticks on your kite.

____

____

4. Put your kite high in the air.

____

____

5. Use your kite with some people.

____

____

Name ______________________________

Self-Evaluation Guide

How-to Report

Directions Think about the final draft of your how-to report. Then rate yourself on a scale of from 4 to 1 (4 is the highest) on each writing trait. After you fill out the chart, answer the questions.

Writing Traits	4	3	2	1
Focus/Ideas				
Organization/Paragraphs				
Voice				
Word Choice				
Sentences				
Conventions				

1. What is the best part of your how-to report?

____

____

____

____

2. Write one thing you would change about this how-to report if you had the chance to write it again.

____

____

____

____

Name ______________________________

Compare/Contrast T-Chart

Directions Write a topic sentence for your compare and contrast essay. Use the T-chart to compare and contrast two things in nature. Write a conclusion sentence.

Topic Sentence ______________________________

____

Similarities	Differences

Conclusion Sentence ______________________________

____

Name ______________________________

Words That Compare and Contrast

Directions The words in the box signal that two things are alike or different. Write two sentences that explain how your two topics are alike. Use words from the box. Then write two sentences that explain how your two topics are different. Use words from the box.

Words That Signal Similarity	Words That Signal Difference
and	but
also	however
too	on the other hand
as well	

How the two things are alike

1. ______________________________

____

2. ______________________________

____

How the two things are different

1. ______________________________

____

2. ______________________________

____

Name ______________________________

Elaboration

Main and Helping Verbs

You can use helping verbs with main verbs to show that something happens at a specific time.

General	Rain helps the flowers grow.
More Specific	Rain will help the flowers grow.
	Rain has (*or* had) helped the flowers grow.

Directions Add a helping verb to the underlined verb in each sentence. Show that each action happened at the time shown in ( ). You may have to change the form of the main verb. Write each new sentence.

1. The weather <u>turns</u> cold in winter. (future)

____

2. Snow <u>covers</u> the roofs and trees. (past)

____

3. Flowers <u>bloom</u> early next spring. (future)

____

4. The sun <u>helps</u> things grow. (past)

____

5. The trees <u>drop</u> their leaves already this fall. (past)

____

6. Wind <u>scatters</u> the leaves around the yard. (future)

____

Name ______________________________

Self-Evaluation Guide

Compare and Contrast Essay

Directions Think about the final draft of your compare and contrast essay. Then rate yourself on a scale of from 4 to 1 (4 is the highest) on each writing trait. After you fill out the chart, answer the questions.

Writing Traits	4	3	2	1
Focus/Ideas				
Organization/Paragraphs				
Voice				
Word Choice				
Sentences				
Conventions				

1. What is the best part of your compare and contrast essay?

____

____

____

____

2. Write one thing you would change about this compare and contrast essay if you had the chance to write it again.

____

____

____

____

Name ________________________________

Story Chart

Directions Fill in the graphic organizer with information about your story.

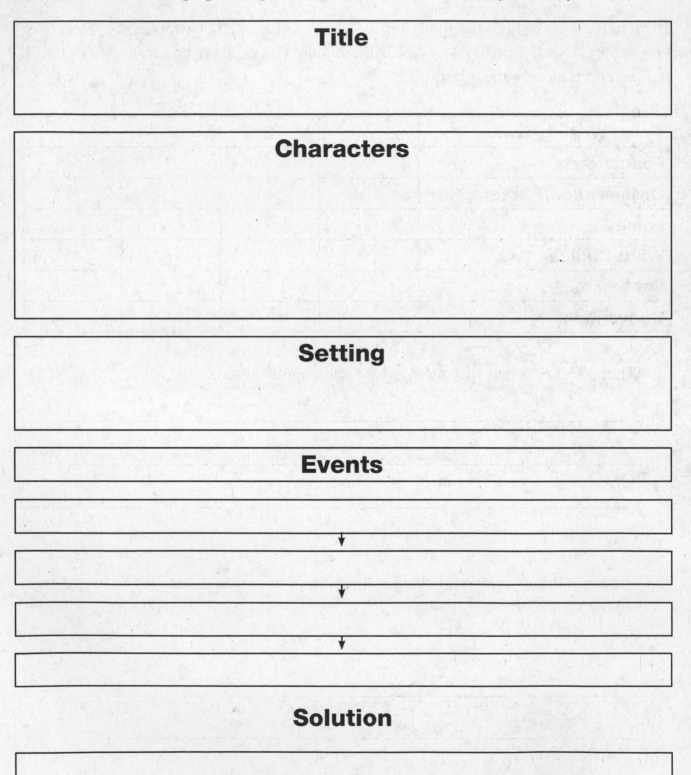

Title

Characters

Setting

Events

Solution

Name ________________________________

Write a Strong Story Opener

Make the first sentence of your story grab your readers' attention. Below are some different kinds of story openers.

Directions Write an attention-grabbing opening sentence (based on your characters, setting, and plot) using each idea. Use one of the sentences to begin your story.

1. **Ask a question.** *(Example: Have you ever heard of a 10-year-old composer?)*

   ____

2. **Use an exclamation.** *(Example: What a talented boy Jeffrey Jackson was!)*

   ____

3. **Use a sound word.** *(Example: Whoosh! Traffic sped past Jeffrey.)*

   ____

4. **Hint at the ending.** *(Example: As Jeffrey walked to school that day, he never imagined being on a stage in front of hundreds of people.)*

   ____

   ____

5. **Appeal to the senses.** *(Example: As lights glared in his eyes and applause thundered in his ears, Jeffrey shook the conductor's sweaty hand.)*

   ____

   ____

6. **Set the scene.** *(Example: The audience waited breathlessly as the conductor raised his baton before the orchestra.)*

   ____

   ____

Name ______________________________

Elaboration

Prepositional Phrases

You can use prepositional phrases to add specific details to your story. For example, a prepositional phrase can tell where or when something happens or is located.

General	David climbed a mountain.
More Specific	David climbed a mountain near his home.

Directions Add one or more prepositional phrases to each sentence to make it more specific. Write your sentence.

1. David bought special boots.

____

____

2. The weather can be very cold and snowy.

____

____

3. Some skilled climbers went with David.

____

____

4. David had food and water.

____

____

Name ___________________________

Self-Evaluation Guide

Story

Directions Think about the final draft of your story. Then rate yourself on a scale of from 4 to 1 (4 is the highest) on each writing trait. After you fill out the chart, answer the questions.

Writing Traits	4	3	2	1
Focus/Ideas				
Organization/Paragraphs				
Voice				
Word Choice				
Sentences				
Conventions				

1. What is the best part of your story?

____

____

____

____

2. Write one thing you would change about this story if you had the chance to write it again.

____

____

____

____

Name ______________________________

Persuasion Chart

Directions Fill in the graphic organizer with ideas for the introduction, supporting reasons, and conclusion in your persuasive letter.

Introduction: State your opinion or goals.

↓

First reason

↓

Second reason

↓

Third reason (most important)

↓

Conclusion

Name ______________________________

Use Persuasive Words

Persuasive words convince readers to take an action or agree with the writer's opinion. Here are some different kinds of persuasive words:

Words that state that an action is necessary: *should, must, important*
Words that compare: *best, most delicious, most important*
Words that describe positive traits: *educational, healthful, safe, effective*

Directions Write sentences for your persuasive letter. Use the kind of persuasive word shown. Underline your persuasive words.

1. Word that states that an action is necessary

____

____

2. Word that compares

____

____

3. Word that describes positive traits

____

____

4. Any kind of persuasive word

____

____

Name ______________________________

Elaboration

Specific Adverbs

You have learned that adverbs tell about verbs. They can tell *when (soon, often), where (outside, here),* or *how (excitedly, carefully, hungrily)* something happens. You can use adverbs to make your letter more specific and persuasive.

General	She looked at the photographs of Puerto Rico.
More Specific	She looked closely at the photographs of Puerto Rico.

Directions Add an adverb to each sentence to make it more specific. Write the new sentence.

1. Japanese people ___ wear kimonos for special occasions.

____

____

2. Sam ate the big plate of spaghetti ___.

____

____

3. Tourists in China ___ walk on the Great Wall.

____

____

4. You must wrap those Mexican vases ___.

____

____

Name ____________________

Self-Evaluation Guide

Persuasive Letter

Directions Think about the final draft of your letter. Then rate yourself on a scale of from 4 to 1 (4 is the highest) on each writing trait. After you fill out the chart, answer the questions.

Writing Traits	4	3	2	1
Focus/Ideas				
Organization/Paragraphs				
Voice				
Word Choice				
Sentences				
Conventions				

1. What is the best part of your persuasive letter?

____

____

____

____

2. Write one thing you would change about this letter if you had the chance to write it again.

____

____

____

____

Name ____________________

K-W-L Chart

Directions Fill out this K-W-L chart to help you organize your ideas.

Topic ____________________

What I Know	What I Want to Know	What I Learned

Controlling Question ____________________

____

Name ______________________________

Topic and Detail Sentences

A topic sentence tells the main idea of a paragraph. Detail sentences give supporting facts, descriptions, and examples about the main idea.

Directions Decide how you will organize your paragraphs. Then write a topic sentence and supporting details for each paragraph.

Paragraph 1

Topic Sentence ______________________________

Detail Sentences ______________________________

____

____

Paragraph 2

Topic Sentence ______________________________

Detail Sentences ______________________________

____

____

Paragraph 3

Topic Sentence ______________________________

Detail Sentences ______________________________

____

____

Paragraph 4

Topic Sentence ______________________________

Detail Sentences ______________________________

____

____

Name ______________________________

Elaboration

Combine Sentences

When you **combine sentences,** you join two sentences that are about the same topic. You make them into one sentence.

- You can join two simple sentences and make a compound sentence. Add a comma and a conjunction such as *and, but,* or *or.*
- You can combine two sentences that have the same subject or the same predicate.

Directions Use the word in ( ) to combine each pair of sentences. Remember to add a comma.

1. There are many monuments in Washington. Many people visit them. (and)

____

____

2. Some monuments honor presidents. Others honor soldiers and other ordinary people. (but)

____

____

Directions Combine the sentences. Use the underlined words only once in your new sentence.

3. Some monuments <u>are made of white marble</u>. <u>Some</u> statues <u>are made of white marble.</u>

____

____

Name ______________________________

Self-Evaluation Guide

Research Report

Directions Think about the final draft of your report. Then rate yourself on a scale of from 4 to 1 (4 is the highest) on each writing trait. After you fill out the chart, answer the questions.

Writing Traits	4	3	2	1
Focus/Ideas				
Organization/Paragraphs				
Voice				
Word Choice				
Sentences				
Conventions				

1. What is the best part of your research report?

____

____

____

____

2. Write one thing you would change about this research report if you had the chance to write it again.

____

____

____

____